DON KENYON
His Own Man

G000244576

TIM JONES

AMBERLEY

To dad (Mick), mom (Pat) and brother (Jonathan) who encouraged my passion for cricket and instilled in me a love of Worcestershire cricket from an early age. I'm indebted to them for this.

First published 2015

Amberley Publishing
The Hill, Stroud
Gloucestershire, GL5 4EP

www.amberley-books.com

British Library Cataloguing in Publication Data.
A catalogue record for this book is available from the British Library.

ISBN 978 1 4456 4756 2 (print)
ISBN 978 1 4456 4757 9 (ebook)

Typesetting and Origination by Amberley Publishing.
Printed in the UK.

Contents

Foreword *by Phil Neale*

My first representative game for Worcestershire was for the Second XI in July 1972 against Derbyshire at Stourbridge's ground in Amblecote. At the time I did not appreciate the significance but I soon came to learn that it was the 'home' of one of the county's most influential cricketers, Don Kenyon.

When I made my first-class debut in 1975, Don sat on the general committee at New Road, I therefore got to know him in that capacity and later came to value his wise counsel even more when I was captain and he was president from 1986 to 1989. Like Don, I was fortunate enough to captain back-to-back Championship-winning sides.

It's with great delight and pleasure that Tim has asked me to write the forward to *Don Kenyon: His Own Man*, which celebrates the life and achievements of one of Worcestershire's 'golden greats.'

It has been meticulously researched and details the career of a private, family man and a cricketer destined for greatness from a very early age. Newspaper articles from the 1930s underscore the prowess of the young batsman which was ultimately to bear fruit by playing, albeit too briefly, in the Test arena.

Don is ever associated as the captain of our first Championship winning side in 1964. It's no coincidence that in 1965, having missed several games because of test selection duty, Don returned to inspire the team to a second successive Championship win by captaining them to victory in ten of the eleven remaining games ... with just 7 minutes of the season to spare.

I found Don to be incredibly supportive of me in cricket committee meetings. He would back me to the hilt and was always prepared to see my point of view and support it. He always believed the captain should get what he wants and as a result he placed great faith in me which was hugely rewarding. He understood that the game had changed from 'his day' and had to be played slightly differently, although one telling comment from him, which still resonates with me today, was that 'the basics never change; you just manage your players and get the best out of them'.

Don was never one to throw that past at me, quite the opposite, he was a forward thinker on the game. *His Own Man* is punctuated with references to newspaper articles when Don comments about the structure of the game, dwindling attendances, the advent of one-day cricket and the financial difficulties faced by many counties. Interestingly, these remain 'hot' topics today.

Packed with anecdotes from many former teammates, colleagues and opponents, his family also reveal what he was like as a husband, father and grandfather who did everything within his capability to provide for them. He did it his way and with total belief and conviction in his actions.

Backed up with some rare photographs from Don's own collection, I have no doubt that you will find this nostalgic look back over his career both revealing and compelling.

Phil Neale, 2015

Chapter 1

Retirement, a First Wicket and Going Dutch

Don Kenyon was his own man. He did things his way and never swayed from what he believed to be right, personally or professionally. Typical of the man was his final season, his final game and his final innings.

Following a glittering career, Don's announcement to retire was made in The *Worcester Evening News* on Friday 30 June 1967. Don was meticulous with his record keeping and never threw anything out, including the billboard poster announcing his decision to stop playing.

Local journalist Jack Godfrey, who penned the article, went on to say,

Don Kenyon, Worcestershire's most successful captain in the club's sixty-eight years of first class cricket, today announced his retirement.

Kenyon led Worcestershire to their first Championship success in 1964 and repeated the feat in 1965. Yorkshire pipped the County for the hat trick last year,

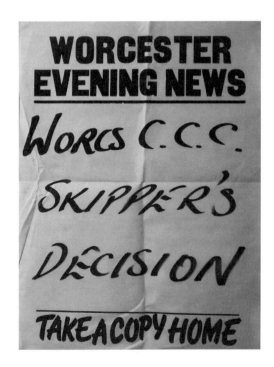

Worcester Evening News flyer announcing Don's retirement, 30 June 1967. From the Kenyon family collection.

the second time under Kenyon's captaincy that the County finished runners up to the Tykes.

In twenty-one years of first class cricket, Kenyon has scored more runs for the County than any other batsman. He has hit 73 centuries and has an aggregate of more than 35,000 runs both Worcestershire records. His top score is 259 against Yorkshire at Kidderminster in 1956.

A most attractive player in his heyday, he has scored 1,000 runs in a season eighteen times and topped 2,000 on seven occasions, being only six short in 1956. He has played in eight Tests – against India, the Australians and South Africa – and has been a Test selector for the last three years.

Worcestershire recognised his wonderful service as a batsman with a £3,840 benefit in 1957, and gave him a £6,351 testimonial in 1964 as an added appreciation of his captaincy as well as a batsman.

Other awards which have come his way in a distinguished career have been one of Wisden's Five Cricketer's of the Year in 1962 and Lord's Taverners' Player of the Year in 1964.

The *Daily Mirror*'s headline stated, 'Kenyon Forty-Three, to Quit Cricket', however, the interesting postscript to the article gave an insight into the way cricket was changing and what the future had in store. It stated, 'The Dean and Chapter of Worcester have agreed to Worcester's request for Sunday cricket in 1968. The cathedral authority is the county Club's landlord.'

On Sunday 12 May 1968, a Worcestershire XI entertained the International Cavaliers in a thirty-six over game. Kenyon opened against his former county but was bowled by Len Coldwell for a single. The visiting side contained names such as Rohan Kanhai, Bobby Simpson, Godfrey Evans, Trevor Bailey and Worcestershire's Jack Flavell. A forty over experiment was played against Warwickshire on Sunday 4 August billed as the Mackeson Trophy Match. While Worcester got home by 100 runs, these well attended games were a forerunner to the hugely popular Players County League in 1969 and subsequent John Player League from 1970 onwards.

Quoting Don from one of the many columns he wrote for the *Sports Argus,* on Saturday July 1 1967 he said, 'Personally, I think for the welfare of the game that Sunday cricket is a must and it is bound to become general in the next few years.'

These were profound words. The John Player League became a hugely popular format with regular fixtures each Sunday afternoon. Sides would complete 40 overs in 2 hours 10 minutes, something accelerated thanks to the bowlers' run-ups being restricted to just 15 yards. Strange as it seems, imposing a shortened run was the making of Michael Holding and Richard Hadlee because it meant they had to quickly find their rhythm.

There were often packed houses at New Road, with the volume increasing from The Severn Bar as the afternoon wore on. How could you ever forget the televised coverage on BBC Two with Peter Walker, John Arlott and Jim Laker sharing the commentary? Peter Walker's tea time interviews were the stuff of legend where he would pack 20 minutes of spell binding conversation into the break.

The game was about to change though. The Gillette Cup had been introduced in 1963, so the advent of Sunday cricket was the next chapter in broadening the appeal to a different audience. This was borne out later in the season when 10,000 spectators turned up to watch a Cavaliers game at New Road, the proceeds from which added £879 to Dick Richardson's benefit fund. As Don said, 'It does my heart good to see so many people present.'

While Secretary Joe Lister said that the captain's decision to retire had been sprung on the club at short notice, Don said that the reason for his retirement was his age. 'I have made the decision regretfully, but I have had this in mind for some time. I thought I would give it a go for a couple of months to see how I fared but it is too much. I find myself unable to concentrate.'

The *Express* and *Star's* headline stated that 'Cricket loses a prolific scorer' and on Saturday 1 July, Michael Blair in the *Birmingham Post* referred to Don as the phlegmatic killer. With a bat in his hand he was a bully. Even today, when his good innings come rather far apart, he is the supreme killer of a bad ball. He likes a bit of needle in his cricket but admits that he is not enamoured of the way they play the game in Yorkshire and has made the point by taking more runs off them than any other county.

Wicketkeeper Roy Booth was in the unique position of having seen Don score double hundreds against Yorkshire on two separate occasions, the first time as an opponent and the second as a teammate.

Michael Blair continued,

People will talk of those explosive off drives, full of meat and utter certainty; of that crushing shot past gulley and that fearless hook.

The hook seems to symbolise the killer batsman, and that is what Kenyon was best at. He has been a killer, out to show that cricket is a world for batsmen. It will be that much poorer without him.

Kenyon was the phlegmatic head of the operation. But he has never had a reputation as a great leader of men or a great maker of tactics. He just knew his cricket and expected his men to know theirs. When Worcestershire were playing at their very best there was no conscious drive at all. The team just ripened around him.

This quote conflicted with the opinion of each and every player who played with and against Don. Many commented on how skilful his leadership was. How natural he was at inspiring his players and the gift he had and, as Ron Headley put it when I interviewed him one cold winter's evening, to make them 'feel 10-feet tall'.

The great Worcestershire CCC historian W. R. Chignell dedicated his second volume of his club history to Don with the quote, 'Don Kenyon – Leader of Champions and Champion of Leaders.' This quotation is still visible on a brass plaque in the club 1865 Lounge at New Road, formerly known as the Kenyon Suite. Some years ago, following the death of Mervyn Roberts, a good friend, his wife, Dorothy, gave the Club's Heritage Group a donation which was used to frame a series of pictures of Don. Chignell's quote appears on the dedication to both Don and Mervyn.

Don's decision to retire, however, seemed to give him a new lease of life. Just a week after the announcement he rolled back the years, and with the help of Alan Ormrod (75 not out), reached a target of 229 to beat Essex by nine wickets in the last over of extra time. Denis Lowe in the *Daily Telegraph* on 5 July headed his article with, 'Kenyon and Ormrod Earn 110 an Hour Victory', with the headline in the *Daily Express* reading, 'The Gay Don Dazzles on to Victory'.

Jack Godfrey headlined in *The Evening News* with, 'County's Triumphant Chase for Runs – Kenyon and Ormrod Hit 174 in 94 minutes'. Jack Godfrey wrote,

> Don Kenyon strode down the pitch to biff 4, 2, 4, 6, 1, 4 off the last six balls of the Essex match at New Road yesterday to stamp his authority on a pulsating innings.
>
> In a 94 minute thrash Kenyon and Ormrod savaged the Essex attack for 174 runs. The last 121 had come in a pounding of a shade under an hour.

Kenyon stated, 'I always fancied we might get the runs as long as we did not lose wickets, but as for myself I got that bit of luck you need when chasing runs at this rate.

'I went down the wicket and swung with the ball, I was too far down to be lbw if I missed, but fortunately I connected every time.' Sadly this was to be his only century of the season. Don also stated in the *Sports Argus* the following weekend that Alan Ormrod's inning was one of the best he ever saw him play.

Don's last appearance at New Road came in the three day game against Pakistan. The game proved to be significant in other ways, none more so than the first class debuts of Glenn Turner (who opened with Don for the one and only time in his career) and Derek Isles, a twenty-three year old from Bradford. Like Kenyon, Turner became one of the Worcestershire greats.

Tom Graveney commented that Turner would be the batsman of the 1970s and he was proved right. No other player scored more runs in that decade than Glenn. In July 2014 I was able to meet up with Glenn, who was visiting New Road via a trip to Royal Porthcawl to watch his bother Greg in the Seniors Open Golf Championship. Greg finished well down the leader board but a third round sixty-six had added some respectability to his card.

Looking as fit as ever, a firm handshake and warm greeting followed, Glenn then recalled his first game, along with what he remembered about Don:

> I put my coffin down in the pavilion dressing room and Norman (Gifford) politely tapped me on the shoulder and explained that only the senior professionals and first teamers change in here.
>
> Norman pointed out that I was to change in the loft, accessed through a corridor in the changing room and up the stairs at the back.

The old pavilion at New Road had stood since it was built in 1898 until it was replaced with the Graeme Hick Pavilion in 2009. Designed by Architect Alfred Hill-Parker and built by E. C. Walton and Company from Newark, the dressing rooms were designed exclusively for the amateurs to change in.

Opening the innings for the last time with Glenn Turner. © Berrows Newspapers.

The professionals would change in a tin shack at the back of the pavilion and enter the field of play from a separate gate. Although the professional/amateur status had been abolished, Glenn having to change elsewhere was a reminder that status still had a part to play in cricket although it was somewhat diminished.

He continued,

> I stood at first slip next to Derek Isles the wicketkeeper who was also making his first class debut. Don was in the gully, not so mobile in those days.
>
> Derek's wife was sitting in the Ladies' Pavilion (it was not until 1978 that ladies were allowed in the main pavilion, yet another indication of how the game was changing, albeit slowly) and then Don came across.
>
> 'I say matey' – a term Don used extensively – 'who is the good looking blonde sitting in the Ladies' Pavilion?' Quickly we put him right to save any embarrassment and smiled at the conversation we had just had. An ice breaker if ever one was needed!
>
> A pair of binoculars was kept on the dressing room window sill in the home dressing room for one purpose only.

The second debutant, Derek Isles, was to re-live some happy memories,

> The secretary, Joe Lister on the week I was picked to play, poked his head round the loft door, and told me and Glenn that we were playing against Pakistan on the Saturday.

The first time I met Don was on the day of the game. I had bumped into him on the training days of pre-season; we played football on the ground behind the scoreboard. I played against Flav, (Jack Flavell) Coldwell and Standen. I tackled Flav on a couple of occasions and was told by everyone to 'watch out; he'll be after you.' Thankfully I was able to avoid that.

Standen was around in goal, he was the best fielder I ever saw. He was used in Tests as twelfth man I think (in the Lord's Test Match of 1966). He was brilliant at third man, fine leg or in the deep; he could throw and was quick to cover the ground.

In those days you were quite remote if not a first team player, however, I got a chance to watch Don at close quarters. He was an aggressive captain, took the odd risk which also applied to his batting. He took attacks apart, he didn't stand back – he attacked them rather than the bowlers attack him.

Gilbert Parkhouse was coach when I went for trials. Having been successful and offered a contract, he left so when I was there, there was no coach. I was left to my own devices. When I was on trial I got to bat and bowl against the first teamers. During one of the trial games Len and Jack were coming back from injury, so they bowled to prove they were fit. It was quite eventful; I must have done okay because I was offered a contract.

As captain he was very much respected by players. He had some egos to manage and did it well. On his last day when we went to field, the first thing he did was to get the new ball from the umpires and throw it to me a few times just to get me in and among them – nice touch.

I remembered Glenn; I played a lot with him in the seconds. He was a part time bowler and Don brought him into action fairly early. He got Hanif Mohammed out, stumped Isles, bowled Turner for 118, not a bad victim to get really. He was a very good player, used his feet a lot but after getting his ton he waltzed down the wicket and I got him.

Michael Blair in *The Birmingham Post* described Hanif's innings as 'bloodthirsty', making his 118 in 2 hours 50 minutes. In today's age of fast scoring, a hundred in nearly 3 hours seems quite pedestrian in comparison.

Derek Isles said, 'Although I kept wicket in this game, in addition to my one catch and one stumping, I was seventeen not out, batting at number nine. It means that I have the rare distinction of not having a first class average even though I batted.'

The game also took an unusual twist for the captain, who picked up his one and only first class wicket, that of Arif Butt, caught and bowled for a single in Pakistan's second innings, and the story was complete.

In addition to claiming his first wicket, Don's other final act was to capture his last playing day at New Road on film. This is something he did extensively when he accompanied the team on the World Tour in 1965. Ironically, Don died in The Kenyon Room itself, on 12 November 1996, just as he had stood up to show the cine film of that magical tour.

Don's final first class game was against Glamorgan at that picturesque ground of Colwyn Bay starting on 31 August he signed off with 67 not out in the second innings to help draw the game, which saw the county finish sixth in the table.

Celebrating his one and
only first-class wicket. ©
Berrows Newspapers.

His career was celebrated in a specially commissioned portrait by Wordsley
artist, George Corbett. With Don proudly wearing his England blazer and with
Worcester Cathedral as a fitting backdrop, it hangs in his wife Jean's lounge at
home as a lasting memory to her husband.

The last game of Don's season was a two day game against All Holland at
the Den Haag ground. The Club's 1968 Yearbook reported on this drawn game
stating that it had 'been eagerly awaited by the players but was marred by wet
and cold weather'.

A small ground, it now offers the most fantastic semi-circular pavilion and
decked area overlooking the ground from which to watch cricket. To the left
as you look out, a stunning medieval church is just a short throw from the
boundary, very much like being at New Road but on a smaller scale.

In 1967, Worcestershire were dismissed for 125 in their first innings and
found themselves twenty-four behind, but thanks to eighty from Don and fifty-
three from Basil D'Oliveira, All Holland were set 217 to win in just 140 minutes.
A Dutch reporter noted, 'To set Holland 217 to win in the remaining time was
an impossibility. This peculiar declaration made the match dead and the fact
that bad light and rain caused an early close of play was really the best solution.'

His own man right until the end, Don had played this exactly as he had
wanted.

Left: Portrait of Don by George Corbett; it now hangs proudly in Jean's home.

Below: Den Haag cricket tour 1967. From the Kenyon family collection.

Chapter 2

From School to Stourbridge and the RAF

Don Kenyon and Jean Corneloues were childhood sweethearts and shared a life of joy and happiness. Don's family was the most important thing to him and he did everything in his power to make sure their needs were always met. Some people say that Don was careful with his money. True as this may be, when it came to Jean and their daughters Lesley and Sue, no expense was spared on their well-being and future security.

Norman Whiting, a witty and entertaining man knew Don as well as anyone. Shortly before his death, Norman relayed a conversation he had with Don very early on in Don's career, 'He told me that, "I have come into this game with nothing but I shan't leave with nothing"; this was an early indication of his drive and determination to reach the highest standard within the game.'

I'd first met Norman on the pre-season tour to the Far East which the players and some members of Worcestershire CCC went on in 1989 and remember vividly one moment which summed up his spirit. I was sitting across the aisle from him on the flight from Brisbane to Hong Kong. A very attractive air stewardess was walking by and as she did Norman stuck out his left arm and stopped her: 'Excuse me my lovely, if you are frightened of heights you can come and sit by me and we can hold hands.' As I was to find out, this was typical Norman in respect of how he charmed the ladies.

Don was born on 15 May 1924 at No. 33 Alwen Street in Wordsley, a village between Stourbridge and Kingswinford. He shared the same birthday coincidentally as another Worcestershire great Jack Flavell who was born five years later. Don's grandmother lived next door and from an early age he would spend hours playing cricket when his father and uncle would bowl at him in the entry to the side of the house.

A cricket enthusiast himself, Don's father was no mean cricketer and played for Stuart Crystal the glassmakers in Stourbridge. Jean recalls how skilled he was as a craftsman who engraved a piece of cut glass which had been made by Jack Lowe, a neighbour, who also worked at 'Stuart's', for their wedding. This is still proudly on display in Jean's lounge.

Don's first taste of cricket came at Brook Street School where he played in games held on the Labour in Vain ground at Brockmoor. Many of his friends were keen cricketers too and they would play games and as Stan Hill wrote in his book *Black Country Personalities*, 'Their games of cricket would last for days, the boys playing during school lunch breaks and after school. Don was nicknamed 'Braddy' – after Don Bradman – as they could hardly ever bowl him out!'

Moving to Audnam Senior School at the top of George Street, for 3*d* a week Don would help the caretaker sweep up. This was an early indication of his appreciation for money; he saved up to buy a Hornby Train set (which is still in possession of the family) with the proceeds. This belief of having to work for what you got was borne out of seeing his father struggle at times during the Great Depression. Don's priority was to support his family and provide the happiest of home environments. He remained faithful to this ethos throughout his life.

At Audnam, Don was also to come into contact with the most influential figure of his burgeoning cricket career, his headmaster, Fred Dale. Over twenty years ago, Don recorded some recollections of his early cricketing memories on an old tape recorder. Here is one extract from this rare and revealing source of information:

Before going to Stourbridge Cricket Club, a schoolmaster friend of mine, Fred Dale took an interest in my cricket. Fred himself played first class second XI cricket and he was the only one in the early days I ever had coaching from.

Fred was very helpful and advised me to go to Stourbridge, which I did. In 1938 I played for the third team and also some occasional second XI games and did reasonably well. By 1939 I got into the first team and during that season had a trial at Worcester. It was during the summer holiday when I was invited to go and play for the Club and Ground XI. The onset of war, however, put a stop to any professional cricket. This stop was to last until 1946.

Brook Street Primary School, 1932. Seated on the ground, second from the right. © The *Black Country Bugle*.

Fred would draw a line on the concrete playground in chalk from the alignment of the middle stump and throw the ball at me. More often than not, it would be to the offside of the line and he would shout 'covers, covers, covers' for where he wanted the ball repeatedly struck.

It was this degree of practice which helped the young Don to perfect his game and many years later, he adopted this same routine, spending many hours bowling to his grandson Daniel in the nets at New Road.

Norman Whiting said,

When I first come across Don he was big for his age, he used to train at Stourbridge FC. He had big thighs and was tremendously strong and was not a bad football player either. He would take penalties and was so strong that he would kick the ball over the stand wearing soft shoes.

It was our decision to train, we'd go in the day, do a few laps around the ground, then have a shower, all just to keep fit. We chose to do it, such was his dedication, but not everyone did. It's about individual motivation.

Don's dedication to his craft was further in evidence as Norman commented once more, 'Bob Wyatt (who was our mentor in those days) used to take a little step back towards off stump to stop himself leaning across just as the bowler was about to bowl. Jean said that Don spent hours in front of the mirror in the winter to perfect this technique.' He subsequently mastered it without thinking, which was purely and simply down to practice and his desire to be the best.

On leaving school, Don attended Brierley Hill Technical College where, among other things, he began to study shorthand and typing. He then joined Lunt Brothers, the coal merchants at the bottom of Brierley Hill High Street.

Jean Kenyon revealed,

The railway office was opposite where the coal was brought in. 'Lunts' then had people go round to customers who paid half a crown a week, Don was appointed as a ledger clerk entering these payments.

At the start of the war my mother went to work there, also as a ledger clerk. She would always talk a lot about her two daughters (me and my sister), and Don and a friend of his would stand outside our house hoping to see us. I asked my mother what on earth he was doing, but she just told me to go out and meet him. I was fifteen at the time and Don was not quite eighteen.

A few years earlier, Don's cricketing prowess had begun to show itself. The *County Express* newspaper in May 1938 stated:

Credit for Stourbridge's home victory on Whit Monday goes to fourteen-year-old D. Kenyon. In reply to Smethwick's total of 132, Stourbridge had lost five wickets for thirty-four when Kenyon stopped the rot.

He and Harris put on 29 for the sixth wicket and when the latter was given out Kenyon carried on with Kitson and the Smethwick total was passed with four wickets in hand.

With the confidence of a veteran, Kenyon hit a four as his first scoring shot and followed this up with two twos and another four. He played with remarkable constraint and discretion always choosing the right ball to hit. It was Kenyon who fittingly made the winning hit.

'Fourteen-Year-Old Batsman to the Rescue –
Bright and Breezy Display for Stourbridge II'

By 1940 he was playing first team cricket. One newspaper stated,

Donald Kenyon the sixteen-year-old Stourbridge Cricket Club player achieved two remarkable batting feats this holiday period. On Saturday he scored 103 for the first team in their Birmingham League game against Aston Unity at Aston and on Monday he made 100 for a Club XI against a strong RAF team at the County Ground, Amblecote.

Kenyon is believed to be the youngest player ever to have scored a century in the Birmingham Cricket League. In all the club's matches this season he has over 600 runs with an average of nearly forty per innings – a truly remarkable performance for one so young.

'D. Kenyon's Two Centuries – Brilliant Weekend Batting'

The following season, the highlight was a score of 103 (2 sixes, 12 fours) when Stourbridge chased down 245 at Kidderminster for the loss of only three wickets with 20 minutes of the game to spare. By now though the country was in the grip of war.

Jean Kenyon stated,

We would still meet up and went for walks in an evening and I discovered that at school Don had been in the Air Training Corps. Shortly before he was eighteen in May 1942 he volunteered, if he'd waited until he reached eighteen he would have been called up automatically to the Army but this way he got what he wanted and was chosen for the RAF

He was sent for a medical and had to go to Weston-super-Mare where it was decided that he would remain. He then had to do square bashing on the prom for six weeks.

His RAF Airman's Service and Pay Book state that his calling up was 8 October 1942. The fact that his book was kept is another example of his meticulous nature in ensuring that so many aspects of his life were chronicled and finely detailed. Don was stationed at Wratting Common in Cambridgeshire and trained as a flight mechanic where he worked through the war on the engines of Lancaster Bombers. His record states (FM/E2) – Flight mechanic, engines, second class. Jean Kenyon said,

I wrote to Don so much, his official number is still in my head to this day, 1668663 LAC, a leading aircraftsman.

He was not permitted to fly; he hadn't received the right education. I recall him mentioning that one night a German plane followed our lads back home and

Above: Stourbridge Cricket Club 1942. Don is seated second from the left, Norman Whiting is standing third from the right. © Coloursport.

Right: In RAF uniform aged eighteen. From the Kenyon family collection.

shot up the aerodrome badly; that was a close call. He always remembered the kindness which the Salvation Army showed to the servicemen during the war and always donated to them because of this.

Sergeant Len Manning an air gunner (rear gunner) flew in Lancaster Bomber number JB318, from 57 Squadron based at East Kirkby in Lincolnshire. He kindly spoke about the work which Don might have carried out:

> They worked in very difficult conditions, not in hangars like you see in some of these old films, but in the open air. There was no cover or shelter from the elements; they worked on a piece of hard standing.
>
>   The flight crew and ground crew had very few dealings together, this was mainly because you tried not to get too close to others because of the chance that you might not be friends for too long. We just had to get on with our job.

Aged just nineteen, Len was shot down on 19 July 1944 at Bassevelle, 20 kilometers south west of Chateau Thierry. Right under the noses of the Germans, he was looked after by the French resistance until the end of the war.

Spare time was at a premium for Don, yet he played his sport whenever he could. A gifted footballer, he was referred to in *The County Express* of 1943 as a 'West Brom hopeful'. It reported, 'West Bromwich Albion are giving plenty of encouragement to D. Kenyon a youthful wing half. Kenyon, who has been giving some fine performances with the junior Throstles, is regarded with as much promise as a cricketer as he is on the football field. Kenyon is considered to be a future Worcestershire player.'

Despite the restrictions of war, Don's cricket career continued to flourish. Playing mainly for his unit, he also found time to represent a team of twelve Worcestershire players against twelve from Warwickshire in August 1942 and also represented the Civil Defence Services, again in a game against Warwickshire. While his cricket was not with the full RAF side, Don's efforts while playing for his unit underlined his great talent for scoring heavy runs, a trait which continued throughout his professional career.

Once again in 1943, *The County Express*' headline announced the availability of Don for Stourbridge in The Birmingham League and proclaimed,

Followers of Stourbridge CC are to have an opportunity during the August holidays of seeing the Club's popular nineteen-year-old young batsman, Don Kenyon, who has been doing some prodigious scoring with the RAF in which he is serving.

Up to 3 July he had batted nine times and scored no fewer than 951 runs. He was five times not out and on each of these occasions passed the century mark, his highest score being over 170. He had the remarkable average of 190 per innings.

'Stourbridge Batsman's Success'

In May 1944 he represented the RAF on two occasions, against Cambridge University and Nottinghamshire respectively. Included in the side which played

Cambridge University was the 'colourful' Wing Commander William Harold Nelson Shakespeare who had played for Worcestershire between 1919 and 1931.

As a pilot, in July 1918 Shakespeare was awarded the Military Cross for conspicuous gallantry and devotion to duty. He successfully carried out two patrols, one in very bad weather and one under intense fire. He flew at a height of 400 feet and brought back very valuable information. Later, he carried out another successful contact patrol at a low altitude, his machine being subjected to intense rifle and machine-gun fire. The citation praised him as 'a gallant and determined pilot'. A few months later he gained the Air Force Cross.

Wing Commander Shakespeare served as Worcestershire County Cricket Club President between 1974 and 1976 and was instrumental in finding Imran Khan a place at Worcester Royal Grammar School prior to him joining the Worcestershire staff.

Former Worcestershire Secretary, Mike Vockins recalls one amusing incident involving the Wing Commander, once described as one of the weakest amateurs to have ever represented the side,

> We were playing a championship game against Leicester, at New Road in 1974, and the batsmen were having particular difficulty in playing 'Garth' McKenzie – a handful at the best of times. However, this day we were facing him on a green top.
>
> The Wing Co. came in during one interval, tore the batsmen off a strip for batting so badly and told them that the best way to play the swinging ball was to take two paces down the pitch and smack McKenzie straight back over his head. I'm told that the players were unhappy to say the least while McKenzie had match figures of 8 – 89 and helped Leicestershire to a four wicket victory.

As the war began to draw to its conclusion, Don continued to play his cricket. On 26 August 1945, the headline in *The Sunday Mercury* read, 'Kenyon Century in 95 minutes'. 'The feature of the final games in The Birmingham and District Cricket League was Stourbridge's fine win by 159 runs over Walsall. D Kenyon knocked up a brilliant not out century in 95 minutes – the only one made for Stourbridge this season.'

First in the Field – A History of the Birmingham and District Cricket League by Alex E. Davis reported,

> Between 1940 and 1945 the Stourbridge side were kept together by professionals like Charles Elliott, Arthur Fitton, John Bloomer, Kenneth Mitchell, Stan Grainger and teenage prodigy, Don Kenyon.
>
> Kenyon took his chance to sharpen his technique against the League professionals so that in 1946 he signed up with Worcestershire to start his eminent career in Test and county cricket.

Still in the RAF, on 18 May 1946, Kenyon was run out for 106 in the Combined Services game against Cambridge and the following week was chosen to make his championship debut for Worcestershire in the game at New Road against Surrey where he was bowled by John Parker for fifteen in his only innings of the match.

In mid-June playing for the RAF against Worcestershire Don bagged a pair for the first time in his career when he was caught behind in both innings by Hugo Yarnold off the bowling of (as fate would have it) Stourbridge cricketer, Leonard Oakley. During his career, Don was to experience 'a pair' on three further occasions.

Don took his revenge in late July when he scored his first, first class hundred (107) for The Combined Services, ironically against Worcestershire. By the time he retired, he had scored a first class hundred against every county (including Worcestershire) with the exception of Middlesex. A top score of ninety against them in that season of 1946 remained his best effort.

On 17 December 1946 Don was demobilised from the forces. His certificate of service and release confirm he was of 'very good character' and deemed a hard working Flight Mechanic (engines). His profession is listed as County Cricketer, a status which was confirmed on 28 February 1947 when he joined the professional staff at New Road and he had completed his apprenticeship with Stourbridge.

Typically, however, his connection with the club remained strong, and he never forgot the help and support which he received in the early days. 1947 was to be his first season in professional cricket.

Chapter 3

Establishing a Place in the Side and a Winter Abroad

In May 1947, *The Birmingham Mail* ran a feature to preview the upcoming season, 'Another Worcestershire player of whom much should be heard is Don Kenyon. He has a fine range of strokes produced with great vigour and ease, and when he has learnt a little more caution, he should make for himself more than a small place in English cricket.'

A bright future beckoned and at this early stage, his appetite for attacking the quick bowlers was evident, albeit tempered with a word of caution. That future was made more certain when the astute Kenyon approached Secretary, Brigadier Mike Green to negotiate his financial remuneration.

Brigadier Mike Green, CBE; MC, was Worcestershire's first secretary following the War and remained in post until 1951. He was responsible for starting the process of improvements at New Road and was especially sensitive to the needs and comfort of spectators. A man of vision, he founded the county's Supporters' Association, something which has continued to go from strength to strength.

Don Kenyon commented,

> Initially my contract was for £150 per year plus match money of £4 for a home game and £6 for an away game. If you didn't play you didn't get this payment. I didn't accept it because I felt I could do with a basic salary. I eventually started with a basic salary of £350 per annum which was graduated up with win money and hotel accommodation.

One of Brigadier Green's first tasks was to appoint a clerk, and following an advert in the newspaper, Grace Fuller (then Miss Cook) was appointed. Speaking to Grace in December 2014, she recalled that Don started playing full time cricket around the same time that she started work. She told me,

> I remember when Brigadier Green interviewed me, he was wearing his forces uniform, he was really great. Don too, was a decent, nice, down to earth man, instantly recognisable by his Black Country twang when he spoke.
>
> He was never flustered, knew precisely what he wanted from his players and carried out his duty as captain as he thought it should be done. He also commanded the highest respect from the players. I remember when I retired in 1986 after forty years' service with the club, he was president and presented

me with a gold necklace and a crystal rose bowl as a token of appreciation of my work for the club.

Norman Whiting also recalled what the early days were like playing alongside Don:

> We used to catch the 8.30 a.m. bus from Stourbridge which would arrive just in time to change into practice gear or playing kit. After the war people from north of the county were mad on cricket and often you couldn't get on the bus. Don's girlfriend's father, a keen cricketer himself, was bus superintendent who, specifically for us during Bank Holidays, would put on an extra bus especially for us, it was a relief.
>
> The problem was getting home; we had no shower or change of togs and had to take our place in the queue. We asked the club for two 'bob' expenses only to be told 'you should live in Worcester!'

Although Don started the season slowly with scores of just two and three, the South African Tourists were beaten by 39 runs thanks to a return of six for thirty-eight from Dick Howorth in the Tourists' second innings. Howorth was to have a memorable season, completing the double of 1,172 runs and 138 wickets at just 16.09 apiece. Mind you, he had to bowl 1,013 overs throughout the season to get there!

With just two half-centuries in the next fourteen innings (64 and 51 against Cambridge University at Fenner's), the big score which had always been around the corner, arrived against the 'old enemy' Warwickshire in early June during the game at Tipton Road, Dudley.

Prior to the game the *Saturday Sports Argus* reported that 'Don Kenyon has not troubled the scorers much, but once he gets going he will keep them busy.' The article signed off by stating that 'within two years Kenyon will be England class. Whether or not he plays, he will be good enough.'

'Kenyon and Wyatt Take Worcester to Victory' was the headline in the *Sporting Buff* on 11 June and stated,

> Whatever honours Warwickshire took at Dudley in the first two days, Worcestershire took back with heavy interest yesterday.
>
> After the loss of two cheap wickets before lunch, with 271 needed for victory, youthful Don Kenyon and veteran Bob Wyatt belaboured the Warwickshire bowling to such an extent that what seemed a tough fight for a draw was turned into a dramatic glorious victory.

Batting at number three, Kenyon made 152 not out, his highest first class score and his first championship hundred. Bob Wyatt (71) and Don added 183 in one hundred and ninety minutes to help the home-side get home by seven wickets with 15 minutes of the extra time to spare.

Wilf Hirst in the *Birmingham Gazette* wrote, 'Kenyon's was a chanceless display marked by some superb driving which brought him 19 fours and marred by only one weak shot. His first 50 took him two and a quarter hours and the second came within 1 hour and the third in 45 minutes.'

Don in a typically aggressive mood against Warwickshire in 1947. From the Kenyon family collection.

The Birmingham Mail commented, 'Kenyon's off driving was sure and profitable and he has already demonstrated that he has the temperament for a crisis.' It had been a well-paced innings which got quicker as the situation of the game dictated. Don built a reputation for selfless batting in the interests of team success, as former wicketkeeper and perpetual Worcestershire stalwart Roy Booth remembered in July 2014.

Roy, incidentally, was the last wicketkeeper to claim 100 victims in a season (eighty-four caught, plus seventeen stumped in 1960 and ninety-one caught, plus nine stumped in 1964). He commented, 'As a captain Don was very selfless. He could have had many more centuries but when he was captain he'd declare to try and win and was not afraid at getting out in the pursuit of a total rather than trying to preserve his wicket.'

Following a six wicket victory – the fourth win of the season – in the game against Sussex at Horsham a few days later, another key milestone in his career was reached when Don was awarded his county cap on 13 June 1947. The game went right up to the wire with the run chase being led by Allan White and Don. The pair added 77 in 40 minutes after what was described as a modest start. Don had scored his runs at a good lick in the attempt to force a victory while *The Daily Herald* reported, 'In the pursuit of runs, Kenyon lifted a mighty 6 into the score box and landed another terrific hit into a hastily vacated deck chair.' It concluded 'an attractive side, Worcester, well worth going some way to watch.' Praise indeed.

Towards the end of July the County began a run of four consecutive wins. While Don had not notched up another ton, he had a series of scores in the mid-forties. To this point he had scored 849 runs from thirty-six innings at an average of 24.25 and he was due another big one.

Another game at Dudley, this time against Nottinghamshire did the trick. While it ended in a tame draw, Don rattled up 102 out of a score of 486, with Charles Palmer contributing 177. In reply, Notts were indebted to Joe Hardstaff for his 202, but yet again the county had Dick Howorth to thank for another five wicket haul (6 – 50 from 30 overs). Although the game had ended in a draw, the attendance at Dudley had been exceptional with 6,000 on the Wednesday, 5,000 on the Thursday and 1,000 on the Friday. The gate receipts for the three days were a record for Dudley at £698 19*s* 3*d*.

While Worcestershire reached sixth in the Championship table, the *Saturday Sports News* for 16 August headlined with 'Kenyon's Promise':

> It is good to see Don Kenyon back in form again. A century on each of his two visits to Dudley has done much to make his first full season of county cricket a memorable one for him.
>
> At twenty-three years of age there are many who believe he has the makings of a really great player. His two displays at Dudley have certainly been refreshing affairs, showing that on his day he has few superiors.

To silence any doubters, it went on to state that there's nothing wrong with 9 fours by an opening batsman in reaching 50 runs and totalling 102. As the season drew to a close, Don's first full year had yielded 1,299 runs at an average of 25.47. He kept his own personal records meticulously for each season he played. Written immaculately in his own hand, he details his record against each county, the venue and the ensuing score along with neatly annotated information relating to specific events such as the awarding of his cap.

In September 1947 Don and his long time sweetheart Jean, were married at St James' Church, Wollaston by Reverend J. R. Bamber. Rev. Bamber served as a chaplain, with the rank of Captain, in the Gloucestershire Regiment. He left England in 1939 and was stationed at a casualty clearing station in France in February 1940. He was ordered to leave France but was reported missing in July. In August the news came that he had been taken prisoner and had been taken into protective custody in May. He spent the rest of the war years in a number of POW camps and was finally released at the end of the war and returned to Wollaston in June 1945.

During the winter Don spent time delivering cars and trade plates for Ted Tinkler (who subsequently went on to play one game for Worcestershire in 1953 against Northamptonshire) and working occasionally for his cousin Geoff Hickman of Hickman the builders. The summer of 1948 promised much, especially for Don in his second season; pre-season practice seemed to have gone well too. The *Sports Argus* in April reported that Don had attended the Sandham, Gover and Strudwick cricket school in London for concentrated practice. It stated, 'I fancy Don Kenyon will show a further advance as a run getter this journey. He has been keeping his eye in and gathering impetus at the

Wedding day, September, 1947.
From the Kenyon family collection.

aforementioned London school. I have heard it suggested that Don is bound to be an England cricketer.'

The visit of Bradman's all conquering Australian side was the first hurdle for the Worcestershire side to overcome, on three previous visits to New Road, Bradman had scored a double hundred. (236 in 1930, 206 in 1934 and 258 in 1938.) The *Evening News and Times* reported that 'even by 6.00 a.m. a small queue was building outside New Road and by 9.00 a.m. there were queues 100 yards long growing at the rate of a yard a minute.' Unfortunately for 'our Don', he was lbw to Ray Lindwall second ball with the home-side being dismissed for just 233. Next day the great man helped himself to 107 as the visitors rattled up 462 – 8 declared with the *Evening News and Times* summing it up beautifully with the headline: 'Bradman's usual Worcester form.' Australia duly went on to complete their victory by an innings and 17 runs. There was much conjecture that Bradman had deliberately thrown his wicket away during the game, something many experts say he would never have considered doing; they are wrong!

A hand written letter of Bradman's dated 11 December 1992 states: 'I had torn a rib cartilage in my last match before leaving Australia and felt some discomfort from it during my innings at Worcester so deliberately got out to prevent any further chance of damage.' The bowler was Peter Jackson who claimed 6 – 135 from 39 overs.

Don's poor start to the season continued. He scored just 107 runs from his first seven innings and lost his place to Fred Cooper for the visit of Surrey in May. He was in and out of the side on seven further occasions and finished the season with the ignominy of 'bagging a pair' against Warwickshire at Dudley. His best in the first team was a knock of ninety-three (run out), batting at number four, in the friendly game against Devon at Devonport in July and a 50 in each innings of the two-day game against Cambridge University. These were his only scores of note.

Glimpses of form had returned but these were mainly in games for the Club and Ground where he would have expected to score heavily; however, his aggregate of 420 runs was his lowest in twenty-one seasons of full time cricket.

In Don's customary end-of-season write up, his notes reveal some interesting comments. Each score is once more neatly written down and a description of each dismissal appears against it:

> Total runs scored in first class matches 420 in twenty-eight knocks, three times not out.
> Scored at an average of 16.8 runs per innings.
> No centuries were scored during the 1948 season.
> This was a very poor season, coupling an injury to the middle finger of the left hand with a run of being off form for most of the season, never once did I settle down in the whole of the season.

Twice he heavily underlined the 420 runs which suggests that he was rather angry and frustrated with his season-long dip in form. Would 1949 prove any better? The start of the new season saw Worcestershire appoint its third different captain since 1946. The latest candidate was Bob Wyatt who was to share the duties with Allan White in what was to prove White's last season. Bob Wyatt had joined Worcestershire after severing his connection with Warwickshire in 1946, he left his mark both as a solid performer and as a successful captain, Don learned a great deal from him.

In *Gentlemen and Players: Conversations with Cricketers*, author, Michael Marshall spoke with Don in 1987 about Bob Wyatt. This interview gives Don's own description of the practice technique that Norman Whiting spoke about.

> Bob Wyatt was a very mellow gentleman when he came to us. He was over fifty when he captained the side and I think he found the atmosphere here a good deal more congenial than he had latterly with Warwickshire. I'm quite certain that everyone who played with him in the Worcestershire side respected him.
>
> Perhaps they didn't all like his old fashioned amateur ways, especially when he had one of those non-jobs as assistant secretary to the county. But everyone respected Bob because he was such a fine player. I spent many hours watching him from the other end when we were batting together and I studied his footwork just as I did when batting with Len Hutton.
>
> We also spent a long time together talking – especially on how to play slow bowling. He was a magnificent player of off spin and the turning ball. He influenced me to get into the habit, one winter, of working on one thing alone.

That was to move one pace to the right in front of the mirror as my first movement until it became second nature. I found this gave me more room for both quick and slow bowling. Reg Simpson did the same thing quite naturally but I learned how to become a good back-foot player by emulating Bob Wyatt.

He maintained his form splendidly right up to the end. I remember him winning a match for us at Taunton when we had to get five off the last ball and he hit Bertie Buse for a magnificent straight six. You'd have thought he was thirty years of age, not fifty.

Don showed promising early-season form with 82 and 71 against Oxford University in what proved to be an encouraging start for the County. By the end of May they had already beaten Sussex, Yorkshire and Warwickshire.

Following the win against Warwickshire, the headline in the *Sports Argus* on Saturday 28 May proclaimed, 'Great Week for Worcestershire but No Room for Complacency.' The article written by 'Severn-sider' also came with a warning to supporters:

> Although I have been in close touch with Worcestershire cricket for many more years than I like to remember, frankly I cannot recall anything to equal or satisfying as the recent deeds of the side. Because Sussex and Warwickshire were well and truly beaten and the champions scared at Pontypridd, there must be no such silly suggestion as the Championship for Worcestershire this season. Yes, I have actually heard such talk. It's just nonsense and does an incalculable amount of harm.
>
> The players know full well the folly of such wild optimism but do those who watch the team's performances understand? I have my doubts.
>
> Yet New Road crowds, I would remind you, have not the best reputation for good cricket manners and they can be readily guilty of maltreatment of home players especially when things are going awkwardly.

Strong stuff indeed, however, for any regulars who sit in, or in front of, the New Road stand at Worcester they will identify with elements of this sentiment, even today. There are occasions that enable the faithful to voice their opinion: if a player is not appearing to give his all, or bowls a couple of loose deliveries, or plays an injudicious stroke. Normally it's good humoured banter, but there are occasions when frustrations are vented as anger and the comments can spill over.

Don's encouraging return to some sort of form was continuing but he was beginning to make the habit of 'getting in and getting out' when in sight of big runs. Frustrating as this was, it did indicate that better things were to follow. Half-centuries against Lancashire (87), Essex (64) and Cambridge University (84) illustrate this well and by the end of June the County had won six of their matches including three on the spin against Essex, Kent and Derbyshire.

The visit of Somerset to Chester Road North, Kidderminster proved to be another thrilling encounter in the increasingly productive season. In spite of 101 from Harold Gimblett and a nine-wicket match haul from Roly Jenkins (4 – 121 and 5 – 95) it was Don who stole the show. Following his first innings, fifty-two, he helped secure a win with one ball of the match to spare with a dazzling 182. Set 339 to win, the home-side slumped to 75–3 before Don and Ronnie Bird set about repairing the damage.

The headlines said it all: 'County Win with Seconds to Spare' 'Don Kenyon Plays the Game of his Life!' It went on to say, 'After having been in a seemingly hopeless position at lunch on the third day against Somerset, Worcestershire won a memorable match.'

The Evening News and Times reported, 'The visitors had left the home-side the formidable task of getting 339 in three and a quarter hours. It was a thrilling race against the clock. After an indifferent start it was a remarkable transformation and Kenyon continued to flog the bowling, one drive for six sailing clean out of the ground.'

When Don was out, caught by Gimblett off Bertie Buse, his 182 was his highest score in first class cricket. Taking just 2 hours and 50 minutes, it contained 4 sixes and 27 fours. It was also his first hundred for two years. Roly Jenkins scored the winning run off the penultimate ball and he and his partner Hugo Yarnold were mobbed by a keyed-up crowd which surged across the outfield amid wildly enthusiastic scenes.

The *Express* and *Star* reported that 'Worcester go to the top once again' and stated that, 'Kenyon took toll of the spin attack and raced to a hundred at a run a minute with a flow of beautiful strokes all-round the wicket.' After fourteen games Worcestershire held a four point lead over Middlesex and had won eight games.

Don received a letter on 22 July enclosing a re-print of their artist's impression of him which had appeared in the *Birmingham Mail* on Saturday 16 July celebrating his exploits against Somerset a few days earlier. A lovely memento of the occasion, a copy is shown below and a second one is on display with other items of Don's memorabilia in the atrium area in the Graeme Hick Pavilion at New Road.

The good form continued into the next game against Nottinghamshire, which started the day after the Somerset game. Back on his home ground of Stourbridge Don raced to 64, mainly in boundaries, but then his innings ended in the most bizarre way. Attempting a hook from Arthur Jepson, his cap fell off, dislodged the bails and he was given out hit wicket. Four more half-centuries were to follow that season, two in the same game (79 and 72) against Hampshire at Worcester.

Defeat against Middlesex at Lord's in mid-August put Worcestershire out of the title race but two more wins and two further drawn games ensured that they finished third, their highest position in the Championship to date. It was made all the more sweet as this was the Club's jubilee season, fifty years had passed since the county attained first class status. In July, the jubilee had been marked by a two-day game and dinner where some of the great and good of the cricketing world convened to celebrate the occasion. Names such as Frank Woolley, Arthur Gilligan, Percy Fender, Charlie Barnett and 'Tiger' Smith were present at the celebration.

Don finished the season with 1,360 runs at an average of 30.22 with just the one memorable hundred to his name. He set off for the winter in the knowledge

With the Compliments

of

SPORTS The Birmingham Mail **FINAL**

Caricature of Don celebrating his 182 against Somerset in 1947. © Mirrorpix.

that while it had not been a spectacular return to form, the worst dip in his career had been overcome.

He spent the winter coaching in Rhodesia it was his first trip abroad on such an assignment. On the next occasion Jean was to accompany him, something which would have been of great comfort to him, especially as he could be prone to homesickness and did not relish being away from his loved ones for any length of time.

Chapter 4

Runs a Plenty, Rhodesia Revisited, Laker Takes Eight and a Taste of Test Cricket

1950 proved to be a pivotal year in the career of Don Kenyon. The potential which had been evident since he was a young boy came to the fore when the sheer volume of runs during the summer got him noticed as a potential England opener. The first piece of recognition came with his selection for the MCC in the drawn game against champion county Yorkshire.

A sign that Don's stock was rising was evident by him being asked to sign an agreement to his availability to play for the MCC when 'invited' during the season. Before the days of central contracts, it's interesting to note that his services were 'mutually agreed' and that some form of income protection was made available in the event of injury.

The customary tour game against The West Indies was badly affected by the rain; however, Don opened his account in the game with a vicious hook for 6 off Frank Worrell, who was opening the bowling because he dared not risk his openers in the appallingly wet conditions. An 80 and a 50 in the match at New Road against the Combined Services set Don up nicely for the first championship game against Leicestershire in mid-May. In an un-enterprising game, Worcestershire were left with 241 to win in a little over two hours. W. R. Chignell wrote in *Worcestershire History*, 'The match remained interesting owing to a beautiful innings of 100 not out by Kenyon out of 150 which he made in 2 hours, 5 minutes. As soon as he reached his hundred the game was abandoned with Worcestershire 150 – 4.' A second innings, 108, could not prevent a ten wicket thumping at the hands of Gloucestershire towards the end of May. The *Birmingham Gazette* reported that 'Kenyon's second century of the season, scored in 4 hours 20 minutes, and Howorth's 79, were praiseworthy efforts in the circumstances but the other Worcestershire batsmen mustered only 28 runs.'

Don's first glimpse of the big time came when he was selected to play for 'The Rest' in the Test Trial at Bradford at the end of May. The invitation to play from Bob Wyatt, Chairman of the selection committee makes interesting reading. The fee for appearing was £30 while an allowance of 10s per day was paid; however, players were expected to meet all other costs outside of these arrangements. Included is a paragraph relating to an embargo about commenting on the game; I shudder to think what the response would be to this request today!

Thanks to Jim Laker, Don's Test ambitions were put on hold a little longer. Opening the innings with David Sheppard of Sussex, Don top scored with 7, as

Laker routed the rest for just 27 returning the amazing figures of 14 – 12 – 2 – 8. In 14 overs he had conceded just 2 runs and claimed eight wickets.

Some thirty-four years later, in 1984, I was lucky enough to attend a lunch in the marquee, adjacent to the net area at New Road, to commemorate twenty years since Worcestershire first won the Championship. I spent an afternoon in the company of Don and Roy Booth and presented them with a picture of Don and David Sheppard which drew immediate comment. Roy said, 'That's Bradford ... I can tell by the great big brick wall.' While Don noted, 'Jim [Laker] was a real handful on a wicket offering him plenty of help. I remember Jim Swanton commenting that Test pitches were usually covered for 24 hours before a game and that those at Bradford should have aimed to do the same with this pitch to at least make the conditions as close to a Test as possible.'

Swanton wrote, 'Kenyon lasted longest and played the best, going back whenever he could and showing considerable skill in taking the balls that were missing the stumps on his pads and thighs.' All of those hours during the winter practising in front of the mirror and observing the ability of Len Hutton and Bob Wyatt to play back had stood Don in good stead. Don's archive contains a neatly presented copy of the scorecard from this game, he has even retained the two complimentary match tickets sent by the Yorkshire Club. Spending the afternoon in the company of two Worcestershire greats was a dream come true. Although I was just twenty-one years old at the time, my knowledge of Worcestershire cricket was growing and I knew precisely the contribution these two players had made to our history. In the tea interval the team went back out to the middle, it was evident to see that the players, who all held back, still regarded Don as 'their captain' and were still following the etiquette of allowing the skipper to take the field of play first.

Back to the day job and normal service was resumed during the trip to Southampton for the game against Hampshire and what a game it turned out to be. A first innings 108 described by The *Birmingham Gazette* as 'one of Kenyon's most patient and brilliant innings' this was followed by a quick fire 67 not out which helped the visitors seal an eight wicket victory. Hampshire set Worcestershire 173 to win in 85 minutes and were indebted to Don who rattled up 50 in 23 minutes and shared an opening stand of 94 with the ever reliable Eddie Cooper who finished 56 not out.

Injuries to Eric Hollies and Trevor Bailey meant that Roly Jenkins was called into the Test team for the match at Lord's and Don was brought into the squad as cover for Reg Simpson. Having already scored 1,448 runs at 49.92 there was optimism that he would get a game. *The Sporting Buff's* headline read: 'Kenyon and Jenkins for Lord's. Although Reg Simpson failed his fitness test, Gilbert Parkhouse was subsequently chosen ahead of Don and in spite of nine wickets in the match for Roly Jenkins, England were trounced by 326 runs. The West Indies went on to record two more huge wins to claim the series by three matches to one.

Three Worcestershire victories and two defeats heralded the visit of Hampshire to Dudley, a ground where Don had scored two hundreds previously. The faithful were not to be disappointed as the local hero cracked 163 in the first innings and thanks to 101 not out from George Dews in the second, beat Hampshire by 164 runs.

Left: Test Trial at Bradford in 1950, opening with David Sheppard © Getty Images.

Below: The Class of '64. 20th anniversary celebration to commemorate winning the Championship, 18 August 1984. © Berrows Newspapers.

The next element of Don's cricketing education was upon him when he was selected for the annual Gentlemen versus Players fixture at Lord's towards the end of July. When asked about the perception of professional cricketers in *Gentleman and Players – Conversations with Cricketers* Don stated,

> You have to remember that there was a brand new breed of young professional cricketer coming into the game. I'd only played for Worcestershire Club and Ground before the war at the age of fifteen, but by the time I came back I'd had several years of wartime service and you grow up rather quickly in those circumstances.
>
> The people who had the most difficult time were the old professionals who'd played for the county before the war and who had lost six years of first class cricket. For quite a while after the war, we had two factions in our dressing room at Worcester. This was still an old wooden shack attached to the side of the pavilion which housed both the old and new professionals and some of the old timers felt threatened by the new intake.

In the second innings Don, batting at number four, scored a quick fire 54 in a drawn game. Back in the Worcestershire ranks a fifth century of the campaign (this time 101 in the second innings against Essex at New Road) confirmed 1950 was turning into a memorable season. It was capped off by 155 against Leicestershire in a match won by 177 runs thanks to a ten wicket match haul from Dick Howorth.

'Kenyon, 155, Gives Worcestershire Good Start in Last Game' was the headline in the *Evening Despatch*. It reported,

> Winning the toss at Leicester, Worcestershire, in their last game of the season, kept Leicestershire in the field all day and made up for a slow start by good scoring towards the end when the home bowlers were tired. The leading figure of the innings was Kenyon who scored 155 out of 255 in four and a half hours, his hitting including a six and 19 fours.

Throughout the season, he had amassed 2,351 runs at an average of 42.74 with six hundreds. His consistency was further underlined by the fact that he also struck fourteen scores of fifty or better in addition to his century tally.

A second winter in Rhodesia beckoned and on this occasion Don had Jean for company and sixty-three years later she recalled the trip,

> We set sail from Southampton, and I've never seen so many ribbons being thrown as when we left, and it was something else. We were fourteen days on board until we docked at Cape Town, then it was a train journey of three days and two nights to Rhodesia. Along the track, every time we stopped the natives came to try and sell you something.
>
> The country itself is 7,000 feet above sea level; I remember when we stepped off the train, the sight and fragrant smell of the beautiful Jacaranda trees. What equally sticks in my mind is how they treated black people; like dirt. One instance was when we stayed with a couple whose servants lived in sheds at the top of the

garden; to be honest I felt ashamed. The Post Office was for whites only with a sign saying 'Coloureds Through Another Door'. As I walked the street they had to make way and stand in the gutter, it really was appalling when you consider the changes which have taken place since. Thinking back it was just like the problems Basil [D'Oliveira] encountered.

We were based in Gweru with Don coaching at Chaplin High School, where Ian Smith, the former Prime Minister of Rhodesia, attended in the 1930s. We also visited Que Que for a while, a place where asbestos was mined.

I had previously worked for the Inland Revenue and was based above the Midland Bank in Stourbridge High Street, processing repayment claims and postal credits. It was on the corner opposite Cook's cafe by the town clock; I went there straight from school. In Rhodesia I worked at Miekles Store, an amazing place, it sold everything! Once they knew I'd been in the Inland Revenue and was adept at handling money, they wanted me to work for them.

We went on a trip to the Matopos [now Matobo] Hills, where Rhodes is buried; the other trip which was so stunning was to Victoria Falls. I was amazed by the mist and spray from the falls; it must have been 200 feet into the air. We were given raincoats to walk as close as we could to it but still got absolutely drenched; mind you, it was worth it, the rainbows were breathtaking.

That was my first trip abroad, I was only twenty at the time, and when we came home we were still living with Don's mom and dad at No. 33 Alwen Street in Wordsley, we couldn't afford anywhere of our own.

In March 1951 an article by 'Citizen' in the *Evening News and Times* stated,

Coaching in Rhodesia has kept him in form. Don Kenyon, the Stourbridge-born Worcestershire opening batsman, arrives in England this week from Southern Rhodesia where he has been coaching at the Chaplin High School, Gwelo, an appointment made by the Rhodesian Education Authority.

The mainstay of his county's batting strength last season, Kenyon attributed his success to his first coaching appointment at the same school in 1949/50 which enabled him to keep his eye in.

Judging by the results of 1950, practice does make perfect.

Chapter 5

Kenyon for England and Dispelling Two Myths

After such a return to form in 1950, The *News and Times* on 28 April 1951 previewed the new season with the bullish headline 'Cap for Kenyon? "This year Worcestershire followers are looking forward to more exhilarating work by Kenyon who may well go one better than last season and get the England cap he just failed to reap against The West Indies."'

1951 also proved to be another fruitful year for the bowlers, three of them passed 100 wickets. Dick Howorth (118 at 17.97), Roly Jenkins (108 at 26.04) and the evergreen Reg Perks (115 at 26.09).

The batsmen went one better with Eddie Cooper (1,603 at 40.07), Bob Broadbent, in his first season (1,163 at 36.34), Laddie Outschoorn (1,318 at 32.88) and Don (1,903 at 43.25) being the mainstays. In early May following the low scoring, drawn game with the South Africans, Don set his stall out with 96 and 100 not out in the drawn game against Derbyshire at New Road. The first innings of 96, however, drew some unfavourable criticism:

> Don Kenyon, smarting from the sting of two comparative failures against the South Africans was determined to take it out of the Derbyshire bowlers. But he did it very gently, too gently for either his own interests of those of his side. Such caution gave the bowlers confidence and when after four and a half hours Kenyon, still having to fight hard for every run, was out within four of his century, those bowlers were still untamed.

The ever reliable George Dews came in for some stinging criticism too, 'One had the spectacle of George Dews going in for the last hour, scraping about for 20 minutes before scoring a run and finishing up with seven laboriously scored runs against bowlers who should have been tired and disheartened.'

With Don's hundred in the second innings secured, the *Evening News and Times* write up by 'Umpire' reported that the opening partnership of 196 between Don and Eddie Cooper was their biggest ever partnership with Cooper falling just eight short of his own hundred. Just a week later a second century of the season was completed, 101 not out in the drawn game with Essex. By mid-May Don had already rattled up 487 runs and with eight or nine further possible innings available during the month; he stood a chance of entering the record books. The *Sporting Buff*'s headline proclaimed, 'Don Kenyon Stands Chance of 1,000 Runs in May'. It was not to be and he finished with 710 in the month and concluded it with his third hundred, 109 against Leicestershire at New Road. This was the first win of the summer after five previous attempts; it had been a slow start for the team.

Four more half-centuries in June and July suggested an indifferent return, an assessment which also summed up the performances of the team during that period. Seven wins, five draws and four defeats was just enough to keep the County well positioned towards the top of the table, which was not bad going considering the lack of wins in the first month. In spite of this, on 25 July the headline in the *Birmingham Mail* announced, 'Kenyon Invited to Tour India'. It reported that 'D. J. Kenyon the Worcestershire opening batsman has been invited by MCC to fill one of the last two places in the party to tour India, Pakistan and Ceylon during the coming winter. It will be Kenyon's first overseas tour, but he has been twelfth man to the England team in this country twice, against the West Indies at Lord's last season and in the first Test of the present series'. A separate report stated, 'Kenyon, who was unaware of his selection until informed by a *News and Times* reporter in the dressing room at the County ground, replied he would be available. He was warmly congratulated by all his colleagues who wished him the best of luck on his first tour.'

It's worth noting that the tour party of fourteen had been named a week before and Don's addition, along with that of Donald Carr, had followed. It also meant that the party contained four opening batsmen; therefore, Don would still face competition for a place. The interesting thing about the reference to Don's selection in the first article is the inclusion of the letter 'J' in his initials. This seems to have appeared for no apparent reason; I have seen the proof on his birth certificate and know that his birth was registered as Donald Kenyon. Mike Vockins, the long-time County Secretary, recalled how he also encountered the 'myth of the additional initial'. When asked about 'the myth', he said,

> When Don was appointed as Chairman of the Cricket Committee in 1976, the minutes of meetings, for no apparent reason, started to appear with D. J. Kenyon; it's a mystery as to what happened and why? Somebody once told me he was D. J. (John) Kenyon and for some reason, unlike me, I accepted that. For ages I referred to him as D. J. Kenyon until one day he said, in his distinct Black Country accent, 'matey, I don't have another name'. That sealed it.

The second myth surrounding Don is that many of the record books state that he was awarded the MBE for his services to cricket. His daughter, Sue Jackson, said that this assertion was wrong and that her father never had this honour bestowed upon him. The fact that it was incorrectly awarded to him was upsetting to Sue and her mother, who feel that he should have received an honour for his services to cricket. A letter I received from the Central Chancery of the Orders of Knighthood in April 2014 confirms that the record books are indeed incorrect. The next trip in the 1951 season was to Scarborough for the game against Yorkshire. 'Kenyon Century in Worcester Crawl' was the headline in the *Yorkshire Post* and *Leeds Mercury*, with the local *Express and Star* reporting:

His long innings at Scarborough rescued Worcester from a threatened collapse. Kenyon scored only 36 in 2 hours before lunch and jogged along for another four and a half hours for his century. Don once stopped batting when barrackers gave him the slow hand clap but umpire Emmott Robinson signalled him to carry on.

The noise immediately subsided and the crowd handsomely apologised for any bad manners when Kenyon fell in the late evening by the reception they gave the batsman on his way back.

'Kenyon Rescue Act Gets Slow Hand'.

The visitors had the last laugh when Reg Perks claimed 6 – 29 in the first innings and Dick Howorth 6 – 63 in the second innings to help Worcestershire cross the line by 8 runs.

Norman Whiting recalled travelling with Don to away games but one occasion especially stuck in his mind: 'It was in Don's first car … he was a funny bloke … we were going round an island on the way into Stourbridge and a wheel disk fell off. Every time subsequently we came home he said "we'll have 10 minutes searching" but we never found it. This was to make sure it couldn't be found and to save a bit of money in buying a replacement.'

Don struck another ton in the next game against Gloucestershire at Cheltenham (120), but yet again the press expressed its dissatisfaction at the rate of scoring. The *Birmingham Mail's* headline was 'Crowd Impatient with Worcester – Slow Scoring Made the Crowd Impatient'.

Three on the spin was next up, 138 in the three wicket victory over Somerset at Taunton; August was turning into a golden month for Don. *The Despatch* reported that he topped 2,000 runs for the season; the second time he had done this in each of the last two seasons. It meant that the County finished a creditable fourth with 132 points having won nine games in all. It meant that Don could head off for his winter tour with great confidence from another fine season where he notched up six centuries in total.

Nigel Howard of Lancashire led the side that left for India knowing that they had been termed 'England's second string', seven of the party were given their Test debuts on the tour. Despite indifferent form early on with 78 runs in seven innings, Don was given his first Test appearance at Feroz Shah Kotla, Delhi and batted at number three scoring 35 and 6 being dismissed in each innings by Sadashiv Shinde.

In December 2013 Tom Graveney, who remembers this tour very well, said, 'Don was very much a family man and was extremely homesick on that tour. I should know I shared a room with him for six months … he was a bloody nightmare.' From the grin on his face I could tell there was no malice in what he said, just a fond remembrance for the man he regarded as the best captain he ever played under. Praise indeed.

'Don kept himself to himself on tour, and didn't like spending much money. He was a home loving sort of bloke. As honest as the day was long, you could rely on him for anything but six months with him', the smile returned to Tom's face once more.

Official players' portrait from the 1951/52
tour to India, Pakistan and Ceylon. From
the Kenyon family collection.

Graveney continued, 'I remember the first Test very well. I missed it with
dysentery, but I scored a hundred in the next game.'

At Delhi, Don was not out at lunch but had forgotten to lock his kit away; this
was very unusual as he was very careful and meticulous in everything he did.
He was half-way back down the pavilion steps and remembered he hadn't put
something away so stopped everything so that he could go back and put it right.
He could then continue with a clear conscience.

On 24 November, it was announced that Don had become a father for the first
time. The announcement stated that 'while Don Kenyon is on tour, his wife
Jean is staying with her parents Mr and Mrs Corneloues at Duncan Street,
Wollaston, Stourbridge.' Joyous as this news was, one can only imagine the
impact it had on an already homesick Don?

Jean Kenyon remembers:

By the time Don returned in the March of 1952, Lesley was already four months
old; it was the first time he had seen her. There was no chance of him popping
back for the birth like they do nowadays. At that time Don's work was to play
cricket and mine was to look after the home and not to interfere with his work.
When he was away for six months or so, we would write to each other every day
but once he was back, he just enjoyed being at home.

With a little hesitancy Jean continued, 'It's similar to Steve Harmison, that lad who was in the England team recently. He seemed a bit of a home bird and didn't like being away. Don was just the same.'

Following the First Test, the party headed to Pakistan for a series of two and four day games. On 19 November the players visited the Lahore Model Town designed with the intent to create a 'garden town' based on co-operative principles with the aim to promote the economic and social interests of its members, particularly to plan, establish and maintain a garden town. The players were each presented with a large medal to commemorate the visit, they were inscribed: 'This medal is presented to Mr D. Kenyon on the occasion of his visit to Model Town, from the Co-Operative Model Town Society Ltd., Lahore, Pakistan.'

Back in India, Don returned to some sort of form in the game against Bombay in early December. The *Birmingham Mail's* headline read 'Kenyon Misses Century by 5 Runs – But Shares in Highest Opening Partnership'. While Don had scored 95, he had shared 172 with Frank Lowson, which was the highest opening partnership of the tour to date.

With scores of 21 and 2 in the Second Test in Bombay followed by 3 and a duck in the Third Test in Calcutta, Don was dropped for the last two Tests. Following the Second Test, the players enjoyed Christmas together and, as was custom in those days, official Christmas cards were issued for players to return home to their loved ones.

After three months of indifferent form, magnified by the intensity of homesickness, Don recorded his first ton of the Tour with 112 in the game against Hyderabad towards the end of January. He had waited nearly three months for this moment. Back in England, the *Birmingham Gazette* celebrated the achievement by writing,

> Don Kenyon, the Worcestershire batsman, must have gained considerable satisfaction from the match, recording his first century of the tour and giving by far his best display.
>
> He hit the ball in the middle of the bat from early in his innings and this gave him confidence which has been lacking in his batting during recent weeks. He made some glorious strokes and when hitting put full power into the shots instead of being half-hearted which is usually the case with a man out of form.

The trip to Hyderabad was made the more memorable with a visit to meet the Nizam of Hyderabad.

The Nizam, born Mir Osman Ali Khan Siddiqi Bahadur, was an interesting and colourful character and of some importance. He was the last Nizam (ruler) of the Princely State of Hyderabad and of Berar. He was reputed to be the richest man in the world, having a fortune estimated at $2 billion in the early 1940s.

His vast inheritance was accumulated as mining royalties. The Hyderabad state was the only supplier of diamonds for the global market in the nineteenth century, such was his influence that he even started his own bank, the Hyderabad State Bank, now The State Bank of Hyderabad. On the return journey, a stay of just over two weeks followed in Ceylon, where the MCC played four matches varying from between two to four days in duration towards the end of February.

Left: Don square cuts on his way to 95 against Bombay, December 1951. From the Kenyon family collection.

Below: MCC visit to the Nizam of Hyderabad. From the Kenyon family collection.

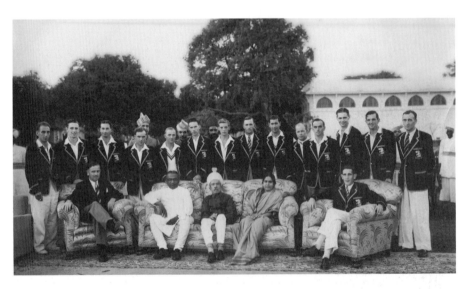

Don's form continued to be poor, in the second game against a Commonwealth XI in Colombo he was dismissed for a duck by none other than Keith Miller, who earlier had smashed the MCC attack for 106 in the Commonwealth's first innings.

Time had now come for Don to return home after a six month trip which had not been the most successful to say the least. The good news was that as the players docked at Tilbury on 22 March, the new season was just around the corner and Don had the chance to meet his daughter Lesley for the first time.

Chapter 6

A Period of Dominance, a Hundred Against the Tourists and Moving House

After six months away from home Don was disappointed with his 'return' of four half-centuries and just the one century from the India tour. It wasn't all gloom and doom though. At the request of editor, Jack Cox, Don was invited to present the four winners of the *Boy's Own Paper* cricket competition with their prizes – A Don Kenyon bat autographed by him.

In May 1952 the Indian tourists were in Worcester, a chance for Don to reacquaint himself with them and to start the season with real purpose. Unfortunately he was dismissed second ball, lbw to Gul Ramchand. Although 3,000 spectators turned up on day one, bad weather meant that the game fizzled out after the completion of just one innings.

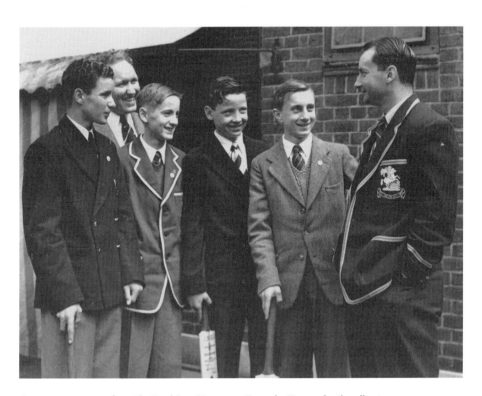

Competition winners from *The Boys' Own Newspaper*. From the Kenyon family collection.

It was not until the last week of May that Don recorded his first big score of the season and in doing so made it two hundreds in a week. They were much needed, especially as the first (109) against Warwickshire stopped the rot following three consecutive defeats. On Saturday 24 May the *Sports Argus* headlined with, 'The Don Hammers Warwickshire'. Charles Harrold reported that 'everyone likes to take a tilt at the champions, and when the top county happens to be Warwickshire and near rivals Worcestershire get them on their own arena, then it's little wonder, with the needle element in the air, that the Severnsiders should hammer Tom Dollery's XI with a vengeance.'

The innings had started slowly. No runs in 30 minutes, 19 in the next 45 minutes and 29 in the 45 minutes to lunch His half-century took two hours fifteen minutes, but he got his second 50 in just 65 minutes. 'Such was Kenyon's driving and cutting when he got going in a remarkable innings of contrast that 60 out of his first 81 runs were scored in boundaries.' Similar to some of his innings during the previous season; a slow start meant that the runs flowed once Don was settled.

A ten wicket match haul from Roly Jenkins (6 – 37 and 4 – 55) helped secure a second victory of the season by 189 runs. While Worcestershire went to Oxford for the three day game, Don found his way into the MCC side to play Lancashire at Lord's. In his absence, his old friend Norman Whiting scored 111 in Worcestershire's first innings, and Peter Richardson who was to become Don's regular opening partner in 1952 scored 110 in the second innings. 'Kenyon Hits Out for MCC' was the headline on Wednesday 28 May. Bowled by Roy Tattersall for a hard hitting 100, Don top scored out of a total of 231 but Lancashire proved too strong and eased past the MCC by eight wickets.

Mid-June saw the third of Don's seven first class hundreds (118) recorded during the season, the Gloucestershire bowlers being the ones to suffer at New Road. 'Worcestershire Hit Back and Kenyon Leads Fight' was the headline in the *Sports Argus*. Even with a slender first innings lead, the home-side did well to hold on for a draw. Set 273 to win in two and a half hours, Worcestershire struggled to 78 – 5 but recovered to 155 – 5 at the close thanks to an unbeaten 62 from Laddie Outschoorn.

A mid-season break for a few days saw the county play two single innings games against Devon at the Recreation Ground in Torquay. In the first, Don was at his belligerent best scoring 198 out of 307 – 5 from just 71 overs in the drawn game. A ten wicket drubbing of Warwickshire in late July ensured that Worcestershire had done the double over the champions. Warwickshire were dismissed for 155 with Worcestershire replying with 280 thanks to a patient 113 from Don in over four hours at the crease. The Club's 1953 Yearbook referred to 'spineless batting' by the visitors in their second innings as they were dismissed for 149. Once again, Roly Jenkins was the destroyer with figures of 6 – 55 and 3 – 56. Ten days later a fifth century of the season (117) against Kent was notched up, however the rain put paid to any result and the match finished as a draw.

The second week of August proved to be the high point of the season for Don. At Trent Bridge the headline in the *Daily Express* read: 'Kenyon, 171 Bats All Day'. Pat Marshall described the innings, 'Dashing Don Kenyon, Worcester's sleek haired, stylish opener, came bursting through a murk of low scores yesterday to record the only century in a day of showery, sawdust cricket. Batting through the whole day against Nottinghamshire, on a wicket twice livened by rain, Kenyon crashed his way to his sixth hundred of the season in two and a half hours.' This was Don at his best!

In the following game against Sussex at Eastbourne, he was at it again with a mammoth 168 in a first innings score of 450 – 4 declared which was in response to the Sussex score of 179. 6 – 97 from George Chesterton and 116 from Captain Ronnie Bird meant that Worcestershire had the better of the game which once more ended in a draw thanks to a more disciplined second innings from the home-side. Kenyon's score was the highest ever by a Worcestershire batsman against Sussex. During the last match of the season against Glamorgan at Cardiff, Don became only the eighth Worcestershire player to score 10,000 runs and at twenty-eight years, 107 days was the youngest at the time.

Another season had come to a close yet it had been a disappointing one with the county finishing in fourteenth place. Don had held the batting together with 2,489 runs at 42.91 with seven first class hundreds in all. While fourteenth was disappointing, the emergence of Peter Richardson as Don's regular opening partner was hugely encouraging. He too scored 2,000 runs while a young Martin Horton was beginning to figure, so there was room for optimism.

In September Don missed out on a hundred for an England XI against a Commonwealth XI at Kingston-upon-Thames. 'Kenyon Just Misses Festival Century' was the headline news, however, the star of the show for the Commonwealth was George Headley with 98 and 62 for the visitors. It turned out that this game at Kingston was one of the first visits of George Headley's son Ron to a cricket match in this country. Here Ron gives an insight of his early recollections of Don:

> The match at Kingston was fierce. On the English side, D. K. was hooking them out of the park. Dad did the same on the other side. He rated D. K. so highly it wasn't true. It was a fiercely competitive game at Kingston. I remember Jock Livingston pulled out a chest pad as he was getting changed, Everton (Weekes) and Uncle Frank (Worrell) found it humorous. Frank Worrell was dad's cousin but he wanted to keep it quiet he did not want to be known as George Headley's cousin for obvious reasons, but I just knew him as Uncle Frank.

In a broad West Indian accent, as if to mimic them both, Ron continued, 'How can a man bat with this on?' He explained that they didn't get it and burst out in loud laughter at the prospect of having to use a chest pad.

> You never even used a thigh pad then and I didn't use one until 1958 – you had to be able to play it off your hip and get out of the way … watch the ball!
>
> I'm a forward thinker but one who was fortunate enough to play when technique was so important. A technique to suit you to play on uncovered wickets – that was the secret of the Don, he played (and played very well) on uncovered pitches. He was a man of great discipline, he didn't hang around the bar at night he was a thorough professional. Cricketers didn't train then, although I used to run a mile and a half every morning from January to April. Nobody knew and

dad said a fit body and a fit mind were secret to his success. I saw dad get 270 in the heat of the sun one day and he talked about the reasons why, it was because he had a fit body and a fit mind.

He used to swim as a youngster 3 miles every morning from Kingston harbour in Jamaica with eight or nine other guys. He was 5 foot, 8 inches tall but they called him Atlas, he was so quick on his feet.

In 1954 when the MCC toured the West Indies, they announced the side Don was excluded. Dad remarked that England have done us a favour, they have made a big mistake; on the West Indian wickets he said he would be devastating to bowl to.

While Don continued into 1953 with further ambition of playing for England, it was a further five years before Ron Headley made his debut for Worcestershire and became very close to Don.

A stern test awaited Don in the opening game of 1953, against the touring Australians led by Lindsay Hassett. A cold and wet start to the season could not dampen the spirits of a huge crowd, even with the early loss of Peter Richardson for a duck. By close of play though the home-side finished on 246 – 3 with Kenyon not out on 117. It was the first time that a Worcestershire batsman had taken a hundred off the Australian tourists. Don had been ably supported by Ronnie Bird (79) who had played the attractive innings of the day while Don's innings in the Club's 1954 Yearbook were described as 'solid and unspectacular'. He was ultimately out for 122, bowled by Richie Benaud.

The *News Chronicle* on 30 April ran the headline, 'Worcester Shock Aussies'. Reporter Crawford White continued, 'England batsmen take note! Don Kenyon and Ronnie Bird of Worcestershire yesterday shook the Australians to the tips of their green caps.' It was the first century scored against them in an opening match of the tour since Len Braund hit 104 for London County in 1902. Ronnie Bird said, 'It was good cricket. Those boys out there were trying all they knew. At least we have shown they can be hit.'

In a later edition, Crawford White's headline made for interesting reading: 'Biff, Bang, Bash for Aussies'. Amusingly, he reported, 'Sir Donald Bradman's ears must have been burning today. For here, where his batting dominated the scene so often in the opening match of an Australian tour, it was the turn of two modest Englishmen.'

The Australians were soon to get their revenge. With the home-side declaring on a creditable 333 – 5, Australia made a very shaky start losing three quick wickets to John Whitehead, who finished the innings with figures of 5 – 89 from 31 overs. Even though they closed day two on a shaky 19 – 3 the Australians need not have worried.

On the final day Keith Miller scorched his way to 220 not out, reportedly, this legendary innings included a six hit into the River Severn. Miller was supported by Graeme Hole from New South Wales who scored 112 and then, batting at number eight, Ron Archer weighed in with 108. At the close, the tourists had reached 542 – 7 in what had been an extraordinary third day.

By now Don was writing a regular feature for the *Sunday Chronicle* and warned against any complacency: 'Don't write off these Australians – Lindwall and Miller are still tops as speed bowlers.' He went on to say, 'I

Norman Edwards cartoon celebrating 122
versus the 1953 Australians. © Mirrorpix.

first played against Ray Lindwall and Keith Miller five years ago, I thought
then they were the two greatest bowlers of their kind in the world. I want
you to know that I still hold the same view. I want to warn English cricket
enthusiasts that this latest Australian side will be as tough a nut to crack as
any other from Down Under.'

At the dinner given by the Worcestershire committee to welcome the
Australians, Lindsay Hassett offered his congratulations: 'It was not easy to find
top form in the first match of the season and a century such as Kenyon's in the
very first innings was a fine performance.'

Two wins and two defeats in the next four championship games evened
things out, Don showed good form with three half-centuries. In the drawn
Bank Holiday game against Essex at Worcester, he scored 120 in the second
innings. Four more half-centuries including a not out 62 for 'The Rest' against
an England XI were doing his chances of a Test recall no harm. The first innings
63 against Derbyshire at Burton-upon-Trent drew a favourable headline from
the *Express and Star*: 'Kenyon Improves his Test Chances.' It stated, 'A four off
the first ball of the day was an indication that Don Kenyon was going to make
the most of his chance. With his Test chances getting daily brightened, Kenyon
became the life and soul of the Worcestershire batting and contributed a well
compiled 63 after giving the team a good start with Richardson.'

It was enough to get Don a recall for the opening game at Trent Bridge.
Charles Bray in the *Daily Herald* wrote the headline: 'Trueman Out, Kenyon
In, and One Surprise – No Jim Laker'. In a low-scoring draw, Don only

England Team for the Trent Bridge test, 1953. © Getty Images.

managed scores of 8 and 16, but then a four wicket win by Worcestershire over Sussex at Dudley the following week served to restore an element of confidence before the Second Test at Lord's.

At the same time, Don and Jean were in the middle of moving house to 'Ken-Loues' in Beech Avenue, Worcester. With Jean expecting her second baby, they still both found time to be interviewed by the *Sports Argus* about their move. It reported:

> The new house in Beech Avenue has for many weeks been Kenyon's main interest behind the cricket scenes. Instead of following the sunshine last winter as he did in the previous three years – two coaching in Rhodesia and a MCC tour to India – he decided to stay in the Midlands so he could set about the task of organising his new garden.
>
> As soon as the roof was on and the majority of the outside structural work completed, Kenyon went to work. What was supposed to be his garden was in fact an old orchard, run wild over the course of many years. Don turned himself into a one man bulldozer and, in the name of good exercise, cleared the lot in the early months of this year.

The article concluded that it makes him a keen gardener by the highest standard!

To verify this Jean recalls, 'Like his father before him, Don was a very keen gardener. He loved to grow tomatoes, loved roses and was brilliant at growing cut flowers like chrysanthemums.'

Mike Vockins said, 'When he retired from playing, Don was just so good with the committee. He brought his home-made damson wine made from his homegrown damsons, it was something to die for – as near to port as you can get. Some of us over indulged sometimes, but he had that generous side to him.'

The pinnacle of any Test career was reached when Don retained his place for the second match at Lord's in the last week of June. Tattersall, May and Simpson were replaced by Willie Watson, Freddie Brown and Brian Statham in another drawn game. Don fared poorly and was dismissed in each innings by Ray Lindwall for scores of just 3 and 2. Dropped for the Third Test and replaced by Bill Edrich, Don took no further part in the series.

The 1953 season continued with an immediate return to form in the drawn game against Warwickshire at New Road. 'Umpire', writing for The *Evening News and Times*, reported,

> As if to emphasise that his Test match form was not a true indication of his ability, Don Kenyon strove manfully to rescue Worcestershire from a bad start to the County's first encounter with neighbours Warwickshire this season.
>
> Kenyon played the bowling so well that he completed his half-century in 95 minutes and when lunch was taken at 103 – 3 he was 70 not out having hit 10 fours. He went on to complete a fine century out of 152 in two and three quarter hours.
>
> 'A Splendid Innings by Kenyon Rescues Worcestershire from Bad Start'

A second hundred in the same week followed at Dudley, where, in a high scoring draw against Gloucestershire, Don rattled up 151 while his opening partner Peter Richardson helped himself to 148 in a stand of 290. It was long-time friend Tom Graveney who, with his part-time leg breaks, ultimately dismissed Don.

Seven more half-centuries underlined the consistent run of form which Don was showing, however, at the end of July he had the dubious honour of being Bob Berry's first victim in the game against Lancashire at Blackpool. It was significant because Berry went on to claim all ten wickets for 102 runs in a run chase of 336 which Worcestershire narrowly failed to achieve by 18 runs.

At Worcester in August Yorkshire were on the receiving end of what was to be a career best score to date. Replying to Yorkshire's 420 – 6 declared, Don batted throughout the Worcestershire innings for 238 not out, compiled over seven and three quarter hours. Containing 30 fours, it was the highest individual score by a batsman against Yorkshire in over fifty years and was the first of seven double centuries scored in his career. Don capped off a memorable season with his last century, 104, in a rain interrupted drawn game against Northamptonshire at Worcester and as September arrived, Don's second daughter Sue was born.

In a season which had started with great optimism for re-establishing himself in the Test team, Don had completed the season for Worcestershire with 2,063 runs in the championship at an average of 47.05 and for the whole season, 2,439 runs with six first class hundreds. Five county batsmen scored over a 1,000 runs, but only the ageing Reg Perks took 100 wickets. Unusually both Perks and Roly Jenkins, missed parts of the season through injury and as a result the County slipped one place to fifteenth, winning only five matches all season.

The Club's Yearbook for 1954 was critical of the bowling but directed its comments to the selection policy, 'It is easy to criticise, but both players and public would have been far happier if they could have known what the policy was that was being adopted. At times there seemed too little, if any, definite policy in team selection. The claim of the selection committee is that their policy was to put the best side available into the field for every match, but in an experimental season that proved to be a short sighted policy.' Would 1954 prove any better?

Chapter 7

Heavy Defeat, Selection Disappointment and a Farcical End to the Season

The review of 1954 in *Chignell's History: Volume II*, does not make for attractive reading:

> Worcestershire rose from fifteenth to equal eleventh, but this was really a rather false picture, for they were actually a weaker side than in 1953. They won and lost the same number of matches as in the previous season – five and twelve respectively and they gained eight points by winning a first innings duel in a game reduced to one day.
>
> They began with a heavy defeat (Pakistan winning by eight wickets in their opening game which was also their first ever visit to Worcester) and finished with a fiasco. In fact they did not win a championship game until July, then they won five of their next nine matches, only to sink back to defeats and drawn games.

With Peter Richardson away on National Service coupled with the loss of form to Bob Broadbent, Ronnie Bird and George Dews, much was placed on Don's shoulders in a thin looking batting line up.

The *Evening News and Times* ran a feature stating that 'these two carry the responsibilities', in reference to Roly Jenkins and Don. W. R. Chignell said, 'To offset the weaknesses Don Kenyon was in even more superb form than before. He was the first man in England to 1,000 runs and 2,000 runs and the only batsman in the country to pass 2,500 runs. Only Jock Livingston, an Australian, apart from Kenyon, passed 2,000 in the season.' While these words of praise sat comfortably, the season was to end in bitter disappointment.

In spite of the team's poor form, Don got off to a flier and recorded the first of his three hundreds in May during the second game against Kent at Gravesend. It had all looked so promising at this stage! In the first innings, which was on his thirtieth birthday, Don scored 60 in three and a quarter hours. 'Handclap for Kenyon Crawl', was the headline next morning because at one point the crowd had been so frustrated with the slow scoring that they began slow clapping, to which Don raised his cap and continued his innings. It meant that Worcestershire took a 30 run lead on first innings, but second time round, Kenyon and his opening partner Outschoorn soon got to work. The *Birmingham Post's* headline read: 'Worcester Race to a Lead of 330 over Kent'. In what was described as sparkling cricket with the batsmen in command, the pair added 277 for the first wicket in just 195 minutes. Declaring at 300 – 3,

Outschoorn had scored 126 while Don remained 152 not out. It all turned sour as Kent reached the target for the loss of six wickets with three members of the top order all scoring a 50.

Worcester had to travel home in the knowledge that the next game started the following day at Leicester. Once more, Kenyon and Outschoorn put on a hundred for the first wicket (145) before Don made his way to a second century of the week, reaching 136. The *Sports Argus* on Saturday 22nd ran a buoyant headline: 'The New Firm Promise a Record Output – Three Matches, Three Century Stands'. It also raised the question, 'Can Don Reach 1,000 in May?' He had raced to 542 runs but with just three matches remaining in May, once again, it wasn't to be.

The next big score had to wait until 29 May, when Don reached three figures again (139) in the game against Oxford University at The Parks which the County won by 11 runs with just 3 minutes of the game remaining. This was their first win in any form this season with the *Daily Mirror* running the celebratory headline: 'Kenyon was a Proper Don at Oxford.'

The local Worcester press, The *Saturday Sports News* known locally as *The Green 'Un* because of its colour, highlighted the problems which many an onlooker was fearing, that the bowling attack lacked any incision. The paper stated, 'They can hardly expect to be great because they lack the services of a good left arm bowler to exploit the conditions which so often rise on the third day of a match.'

Before the month was out, the *Green 'Un* was already putting Kenyon in the frame for a trip to Australia that same winter: 'Don Kenyon is the type to do well in Australia.' Chairman of selectors, Freddie Brown, was also making all the right noises about Don's credentials. In his book, *Cricket Musketeer*, he went on to say, 'Although he failed in his last two Test matches last summer, Don Kenyon of Worcestershire is the type who should do well in Australia. He is an instinctive stroke player and he has the virtue for the faster Australian wickets of not having a big back lift.'

In another drawn game, this time against Essex at Brentwood, the runs flowed yet again. Don raced to 187 and in doing so became the first player to reach the 1,000 runs in the season milestone. Former tennis and squash correspondent, Rex Bellamy of *The Times* wrote, 'After scoring only 347 in two complete innings at Northampton, Worcestershire went to Brentwood to play Essex on Saturday and put on 422 – 5 in six and a half hours, splendid going for the first day of a county championship match.'

Don's innings had contained a six and 24 fours with Rex Bellamy once again writing, 'Perhaps the most exciting moment of the Kenyon's innings was the stroke with which he passed his previous highest score of the season. This stroke was the only six of the day, a soaring drive over mid on from no less a bowler than Trevor Bailey.'

The first win of the season finally arrived against Hampshire at Portsmouth, and what a win it was. Conforming to Worcestershire's new arrangement whereby Ronnie Bird and Reg Perks shared the captaincy (with one resting while the other played) to allow younger players to gain experience, Perks won the toss and made first use of the pitch. By lunch Laddie Outschoorn and Don had added 128 for the first wicket and in doing so Laddie reached his 1,000 runs for the season milestone before he was dismissed for 75. The *Sporting Buff* reported, 'Runs came easily for Kenyon and Outschoorn after lunch against the bowling of Gray and Carty. Kenyon opened his shoulders to each bowler in turn, reaching the boundary with cover drives. The stand reached 150 in 145 minutes.'

When Worcestershire declared at 352 – 6, Kenyon had scored 202 not out. He had struck 27 fours in his innings and passed 1,500 runs for the season. The innings had seen Don at his belligerent best and had scored 44 out of the first 51 to demonstrate just what fine form he was in. The *Birmingham Mail* summed it up with the headline: 'Kenyon in a Run Rush.'

Jack Flavell with 6 – 78 was the destroyer in the first innings as Hampshire were dismissed for just 156 as Australian, Noel Hughes (4 – 19) and Roly Jenkins (3 – 51) were the architects of Hampshire's demise for 180 in the second innings. Worcestershire got home by an innings and 16 runs.

A second win of the season followed against Warwickshire but when Don was selected for The Players against The Gentleman at Lord's the County suffered a nine wicket defeat against Sussex at Hastings. The highlight was a nine wicket haul (9 – 122) from Jack Flavell who might have claimed all ten had Sussex not declared their first innings.

Although he took nine wickets in an innings on two further occasions, these were to be Flavell's best figures. Still we wait for a Worcestershire bowler to claim all ten in an innings, the most recent attempt was from Indian, Zaheer

Players vs Gentlemen, 1954 © EMPICSPA.

Khan, who took 9 – 138 against Essex at Chelmsford in 2006. He would have had all ten not had it been for the normally excellent Steven Davies dropping a catch behind the wicket!

The era of the amateur was coming to an end and the Gentleman versus Players fixture was to continue only until 1962. In Michael Marshall's book, *Gentleman and Players*, the friction which could exist between amateurs and professionals was explored, especially the impact of the captain being of amateur status. Don commented on his own experience:

> The difficulty was not for well-established professionals like Reg (Perks) but for some of those who I describe as marginal cricketers in the side. They were the kind of people who had to drop out when an amateur came in and, if you talk to them today, they are still ticking away on the subject.
>
> Although people like Charles Palmer and George Chesterton were good enough to hold their place in the side, occasionally we included amateurs who weren't quite up to it and that did cause resentment. When it came to the captaincy, the same situation applied.

Some years ago Dave Bradley, a local broadcaster with BBC Hereford and Worcester Radio interviewed Jack Flavell on this subject. Being known for his fiery temperament and forthright views, Jack did not hold back. He was vocal in asking why he should stand down just because someone wanted a game from time to time? As a professional sportsman he could not equate with having to stand down, even if he was not playing well, to give someone else an opportunity.

While the match was supposed to be a barometer to selection for the upcoming tour, Crawford White of the *News Chronicle* wrote of his indifference towards the fixture: 'Fighting Bill Edrich topped the batting poll; Don Kenyon hit yet another half-century; young Peter Loader took three quick wickets; amateur Robin Marlar struck a rich vein of 6 – 20 in the after lunch rout of our cricket professionals; Colin Cowdrey and Jim Parks failed.' Crawford White signed off by saying that 'as a game this classic of the cricket season is evenly poised. As a guide to Australia it must be written off – or at most treated with extreme caution. The problem had been the inability of the authorities to replicate as closely as they could the Australian covered wicket conditions and instead allow the game to be played on a pitch, which, affected by rain, popped, flew and turned from day one.'

The omens were looking good for Don, not just based on this performance and his form to date. The *News Chronicle* ran a postcard ballot to name the seventeen for Australia, Don getting overwhelming public support to make the trip. His return to the Worcestershire ranks helped them regain the winning habit, this time defeating Derbyshire by four wickets at Worcester which was followed up by another double century also at home against Leicestershire at New Road.

The Leicestershire game saw Don at the height of his powers once Jack Flavell (5 – 63) had reduced the visitors to 129 all out. Another century opening stand of 231 with Laddie Outschoorn, (112) and a second wicket stand of 160 with George Dews (83) allowed the home-side to declare on 482 – 2.

Don's contribution was 253 not out. In scoring it he passed 2,000 runs for the season and had bettered his season's highest score, something which he had hit just a few weeks earlier. The *Birmingham Gazette* referred to it as 'Kenyon's match' such was the colossal effort he had put into his score. Don's feats were not going unnoticed. Gerald Nabarro, the MP at the time for Kidderminster even suggested that a congratulatory telegram be sent to Don by the residents of Wolverley, near to Kidderminster, by way of congratulation. It was duly delivered.

The response to Don's innings also prompted many letters to various newspapers across the country begging 'why is Don Kenyon the most prolific scorer this season kept out of Test matches?' 'Why do Graveney and Edrich get so many chances and Kenyon is overlooked?' 'What else does Kenyon have to do to get back in the England side?' One irate letter in particular stated, 'What an insult it is that Kenyon is overlooked.' A pertinent statement, especially as the selection of the tour party was about to be announced in late July.

The score of 253 and Don's volume of runs was even threatening one of Worcestershire's long time records held by 'Doc' Gibbons. He was known as 'Doc' because of his neat appearance and black bag in which he carried his kit which gave him the appearance of a doctor. His season's aggregate of 2,654 runs (at 52.03) with eight centuries set in 1934 was in Don's sights. On 24 July the tour party was announced and to everyone's surprise, Don was omitted. Yet again the newspapers were asking why he had not been included. 'What More Must the Don Do?' and 'Why was Kenyon Left Out?' were just two of the eye catching headlines.

The *Evening Despatch* ran an article titled 'This Tour Choice Doesn't Make Sense' and the Dick Knight column was quoted as saying:

> Two minutes silence please. Hopes of cricketing honours coming the way of Warwickshire and Worcestershire in Australia this winter were smashed yesterday when the MCC's touring party was announced without the names of Don Kenyon, Peter Richardson and Dick Spooner.
>
> Surely there must be alarm when selectors fail to pick the man who is far and away the most successful batsman of the season; I mean Don Kenyon.

It concluded with an even more damning assessment, 'A few days ago a writer asked this column whether anyone could inform him of the qualifications needed for a Test or touring side. I think I can now tell him. The most important qualification of course is to belong to a glamorous Club. It is, therefore, out of the question for a player from Worcestershire to be considered.' Strong words, but the sentiment was shared by many cricket followers around the Midlands. Worcestershire were to win just one more match in the season and the bad news Don received seemed to impact on his scores, with just three more half-centuries to his name throughout August.

In a ten day period, Worcestershire also suffered two heavy defeats at the hands of Surrey. Following a ten wicket hammering at New Road, the season descended into a fiasco with the return game at The Oval. Due to rain, less than the equivalent of a full day's play was needed to conclude the game.

Dismissed for 25 in just a 107 minutes, Worcestershire were left surprised when Surrey skipper Stuart Surridge declared the home-side's first innings on 92 – 3. The visitors subsided to 40 all out to lose by an innings and 27 runs. Worcestershire's aggregate of 65 is still the lowest in the Club's history, and Hugo Yarnold with 14 not out in the second innings was the only Worcestershire player to reach double figures in the game.

Don's season's tally in the championship was 2,138 runs at 53.45 with five centuries and although he had not been able to eclipse 'Doc' Gibbons, he had come close. Despite the fact that his omission from the tour party was a disappointment his wife Jean puts it into perspective:

> Although cricket was his work, me and the family were more important to him, it gave him a real sense of perspective. He was like a bank manager really; when he came home he would not discuss his customers' business, (cricket in Don's case) his work stayed away from the home environment.
>
> When the children were young we bought a caravan in Barmouth and would spend most of August away living there. If Don was playing at Worcester he would finish play on a Saturday, drive through the evening or night to spend Sunday with us. He'd be up at the crack of dawn to get back in time for start of play on the Monday but he thought nothing of it. We were more important than the cricket.

Chapter 8

Another Tilt at England

As the winter of 1955 drew to a close, a new era was underway as an old one came to an end. Reg Perks in his last season was appointed the first professional captain in the Club's history. Towards the end of the season Reg was to announce his retirement having taken 100 wickets in the season for the sixteenth consecutive time; he was forty-three. Reg's career had spanned twenty-five years following his debut against Surrey at The Oval in 1930. It's hard to understand why he only played two Test matches, one of which was the famous timeless Test at Durban in 1938/39. A great servant of Worcestershire cricket, he remains the only man to have taken 2,000 first class wickets for the County.

Don began 1955 by opening for the MCC against Yorkshire at Lord's. His two scores of 14 and 21 were nowhere near enough to prevent an innings and 15 run defeat. First up at New Road were the touring South Africans. Having won the toss and deciding to bat, Worcestershire soon lost Peter Richardson for a duck but after that, the dependable pair of Kenyon and Outschoorn began to repair the early damage. By lunch they had added 95 with The *Saturday Sports News* reporting that 'after the interval Kenyon reached his 50 with a sparkling off drive to the rails, both batsmen looking happy enough with their efforts.'

With the partnership on 113, Don was lbw to the dangerous Peter Heine for 58 leaving Outschoorn to continue the good work until he was caught by 'Jack' Cheetham off Hugh Tayfield for 80. Tayfield had connections with Worcestershire, his uncle Syd Martin had played for the County with great distinction from 1931 until the outbreak of war. A good all-rounder, Syd scored 1,000 runs in a season on six occasions, and claiming 100 wickets in the season twice. His best year was 1937 when he did the double and was one of four bowlers to take 100 wickets that season. Reg Perks, Dick Howorth and Peter Jackson were the others.

In reply to Worcestershire's 260, the visitors could only muster 209 thanks to a spell of 5 – 60 from Bob Berry but with a second five wicket haul from Tayfield (5 – 81) Worcestershire could only set the visitors 261 to win. The tourists were dismissed for just 143, Martin Horton, who had made his debut three years earlier, claimed second innings figures of 9 – 56 to help the home-side open with a win by 117 runs. These remained career best figures for Martin whose contribution meant that Worcestershire were the only county side to inflict a defeat on the tourists during the season.

Martin Horton became a lifelong friend of Don Kenyon, and as his opening partner too, they were inseparable friends on and off the pitch. Martin, a stalwart of the club, played a huge part in the team's success of the 1960s. Before play started on a glorious summer's day at New Road in 2014, Martin's widow Margaret spoke about their enduring friendship: 'In his will Martin wanted his ashes scattering next to Don's, which was a great indication of the strength of their friendship. Don was a lovely man, serious in lots of ways but very much like Martin; they loved their family and cricket and were very respectful of the game.' With a smile Margaret continued,

> Martin said he'd play for nothing if he could – it was his first love; I knew I was second, he never wanted to do anything else.
>
> Both were very stubborn men, if their mind was made up that was it; they were very alike in temperament, that's why they got on so well. Martin was with Don when he died. Don was talking to me, went to the front of the room to talk to The Cricket Society meeting about the World Tour of 1965 and to show his cine film and he just went down. Martin went in the ambulance with him but he died on the way to hospital.
>
> It knocked Martin for six but he knew Don had died how he wanted to – with the people he wanted to be with, no lingering illness, he just died on the spot. He'd got a bad heart, but how wonderful for the person to die without suffering a lingering illness. We had a wonderful life, cricket gives so much as Jean would know. You make friends for life

How true and poignant these words are.

In the last week of May, Worcestershire were securing a first win of the season, a 197 run victory over Scotland at Glasgow. Two half-centuries from Don were a contributing factor, but George Dews (105) and Bob Broadbent (106) who were the top scorers in the game, made the significant contributions.

Speculating in his column in the *Birmingham Mail* on Saturday 21 May, about the make-up of the England side, Don signed off by welcoming a young trialist to New Road, a twenty-two year old medium-fast right armer by the name of Len Coldwell. Len's arrival at the ground was quite dramatic. Recommended by Eddie Cooper, he failed to arrive from Devon at the time arranged by Secretary Major Bayly who wrote him off as another 'couldn't care less' type who did not fulfil his engagements. When net practice was well underway, a figure was seen walking into the ground – a figure with a number of cuts and abrasions. It was Len Coldwell who had had an accident on the way up. Profuse apologies for being late, he refused to go and rest and said he would like to bowl in the nets. He then proceeded to bowl several eminent batsmen including Don. Len insisted that he did not even know it was Don.

Len Coldwell was another player who became one of the greats of Worcestershire cricket, he too figured extensively in the Championship winning years of the 1960s. Some years ago I used to holiday in Teignmouth in Devon with my parents. Sitting in The Pickwick coffee shop one day, my dad noticed Len walking into Dart and Partners the estate agents in Teignmouth

Opening the
batting with
long-time friend,
Martin Horton.
© Coloursport

Triangle. He was definite in his identification so the next time we visited, I took
a picture with me, popped into the shop and got Len to sign it.

I remember that I was thrilled to bits to see it and to talk about his playing
days. He called over two colleagues and said, 'See, I told you I could play cricket
a bit, and what a handsome chap I was too in those days. Look at the braced
left leg, that's how to bowl properly.' As a young collector of memorabilia and
autographs, this had been a triumph to meet such a giant of Worcestershire
cricket and is something I remember to this day.

Don's first ton of the season came against Leicestershire in the game at
Dudley, a ground where he had scored well previously. It was his third century
in consecutive innings against the visitors; his three and a half hour innings
contained seventeen boundaries. Poor weather meant the game ended in a
draw but it was not until 8 July that Worcestershire won their first match of the
season; it proved to be a long wait.

Speculation was also rife about the selection of the England team for the First
Test at Trent Bridge with L. N. Bailey of *The Star* commenting that 'it's been said
that Kenyon lacks the Test temperament but when I was at Worcester for the South
Africans' opening game I had a talk with his county captain, Reg Perks, about this.'

Reg Perks said, 'It is all a lot of rot about Kenyon not having the temperament.
All he needs are the same sort of chances which have been given to other players
in the England team.' This was identical to the comment raised at the end of the
previous season when Don missed out on selection for the Australian tour. And
so it was, Don was recalled to the team for the game starting on 9 June.

Quoted in the *Birmingham Gazette*, Don stated, 'I'm very thrilled to be playing. You can depend on me to try my hardest to justify myself and the selectors.' Opening with new partner Tom Graveney they put on 91 for the first wicket before Graveney was out for 42. The *Daily Sketch* ran the headline: 'Kenyon Arrives to Celebrate What Proved to be his Highest Test Score of 87'. Brian Chapman writing for the *Daily Mirror* went a stage further to proclaim: 'Now Don Kenyon is a Test champion.'

England's first innings of 334 proved too much for South Africa. Wardle with 4 – 24 in the first innings and Tyson with 6 – 28 in the second ensured that England were victorious by an inning and 5 runs. On his return to normal duties Don, writing for the *Birmingham Mail* in 'Don Kenyon's Corner', commented, 'First of all let me say how bucked I was at getting a few runs in the Test match at Nottingham. By MCC regulations I am not allowed to comment on the game itself, so my readers will have to be satisfied with the one outstanding thought in my mind – that those runs were very sweet to me.'

Don retained his place for the Second Test at Lord's on 23 June but scores of 1 (bowled by Neil Adcock) and 2 (lbw to Trevor Goddard) contributed little to England's 71 run victory. A return to some sort of form was in evidence during the Middlesex game at Worcester, a first innings 65 showing signs that another century was not far away. Unfortunately the County were to lose by eight wickets thanks to a match haul of ten wickets from Fred Titmus and a second innings 56 not out from Bill Edrich.

Don was left to hope during the pre-Third Test dinner that after the encouraging score at Trent Bridge a good innings at Old Trafford would cement his place.

Sadly the score he craved did not materialise. Once again Peter Heine claimed Don's wicket, having him caught behind by John Waite in each innings for scores of just 5 and 1. Three South African and two English batsmen had scored centuries in the game, so the writing, once more, was on the wall for Don and his place was again under threat. It proved to be his last innings as a Test cricketer.

I have asked many knowledgeable players on the game why Don did not have a more successful career as a Test player. This was something I was curious to understand, especially considering the volume of runs he scored at County level. Maybe comparisons can be drawn to the more modern era where a similar criticism was levelled at Graeme Hick. Was it ability or temperament which held them both back? Roy Booth stated,

There were a load of opening batsmen around at the time, George Emmett, Reg Simpson, Cyril Washbrook and Len Hutton so there was competition for a place. He also played against Heine and Adcock plus Miller and Lindwall, so there are two great bowling opening partnerships for starters.

The best bowlers were about then; today they play against some powder puff bowling as I call it! It was a different era then, just look who was about for England, some top opening bowlers – Tyson, Statham, Fred, Peter Loader, Jeff Jones. Usually we played against a top class bowler in every team, but as for Don, I don't think he had a fair chance.

Right: Signed menu from pre-Test match dinner at Old Trafford, 1955. From the Kenyon Family collection.

Below: Caught Waite, bowled Heine for 5. Old Trafford Test, 1955. © Getty Images.

I asked former Worcestershire quick bowler, John Aldridge, the same question,

> If he'd played more against New Zealand or India he would have got lots of runs.
> Wes Hall was only just coming through for the West Indies, so they were not yet a
> force to be reckoned with.
>
> Don was sure of his ability which is why it surprises me that he didn't score more
> Test runs, especially as he took the quicks apart. He would say: 'If you see me hit
> one off the back foot through the covers you can back me for a hundred.' He was
> that good.

Duncan Fearnley said, 'There were a lot of good 'uns about then. Like now, if
you get in at the right time, you get a good chance if not, you can struggle.
Look at the opportunity Stokes had with Trott coming home from Australia,
he's grasped it with both hands. Sometimes it's a matter of right time, right place
and nothing more than that.'

There was a fascinating opinion from Raymond Illingworth, someone who
respected Don as an opponent and as a player, 'I remember that in 1955 Lord's
gave a directive that they wanted quicker pitches with grass left on them. In the
First Test at Trent Bridge you couldn't tell the square from the wicket. He had to
go in first against Heine and Adcock and it was really hard to score. Although
he got 80 odd, it was wrong place, wrong time for him.'

Len Hutton, in his book *Just My Story*, stated,

> Despite the sharp division of opinion on the merits of Don Kenyon as a Test
> opening batsman he had retained his place for the match at Lord's, but his failures
> there made me think that to that point he had not acquired the right temperament
> for Test cricket.
>
> Those who disagreed with me before the Lord's Test could now see things
> my way, and the decision was taken to bring back Bill Edrich for Manchester, a
> decision I particularly welcomed, as I had always admired the qualities of Bill
> Edrich as a cricketer.

Worcestershire's long-awaited first win of the season came against
Nottinghamshire at Kidderminster on 19 July by the margin of 117 runs thanks
to a ten wicket match haul from Reg Perks (10 – 123). The batting was not firing,
however, 58 from Don had been some form of contribution, something he took
into the game against Sussex at Hove later in the month. Out for 94, the *Evening
News* reported that 'Don keeps missing out'. Their story reported, 'So near
and yet so far! These days Worcestershire's Don Kenyon must be feeling like a
kindred soul because down at Hove he got into the nineties for the third time
this season without scoring a ton.' The tide eventually turned in late August
when Don rattled up four hundreds in the final month of the season.

Firstly there was 108 in the second innings of the exciting run chase against
Gloucestershire at New Road which secured a win with just 5 minutes to spare.
The other encouragement had been a maiden first class century (126) by Dick
Richardson (younger brother of Peter) in the first innings.

Don followed this with 131 in the first innings of the Leicestershire game but Worcestershire were defeated by five wickets. It was three in three games when the County visited Bournemouth where Hampshire won by 79 runs. In a rear-guard action, Don carried his bat for the only time in his career to finish 103 not out as Worcestershire fell short of their 295 target by 79 runs. The *Birmingham Gazette* reported that 'Kenyon finishes with 103 not out but Worcestershire are beaten.' The report stated, 'In hitting 14 fours, Kenyon passed the 2,000 run mark for the season, but Worcestershire lost their last five wickets for nineteen runs with Reg Perks bagging a pair in his last match.'

The defeat meant that Worcestershire finished in a poor fifteenth place with just five wins and seventeen defeats to show for a summer's work. Surrey retained the title with 200 more points and eighteen more wins.

Batting at number three, Don concluded the summer with 117 for an England XI against a Commonwealth XI during the Torquay Festival at the start of September. After a slow start followed by a series of fifties, the hundreds which had threatened finally arrived. In all, he had scored 1,637 runs in the championship, 2,296 overall and notched up another five centuries. There was no place in the Tour party to Australia, and so it was back to normality during the winter.

It was at this time that he started a long and happy association with Dudley Iron and Steel Company for whom he worked for many years. Taking time to fully understand the steel stockholding business Don carved out a second career and struck up a long-time friendship with managing director Harry Willets.

Jean Kenyon described how accommodating Harry was in the summer to allow Don to play cricket, but that he knew having a well-known cricketer on his books was equally good for trade. Don never forgot this kindness and would invite Harry and his colleagues from Dudley Iron and Steel to spend time in one of the hospitality boxes at Lord's each summer by way of a thank you.

Chapter 9

Change of Captaincy, Forward Thinking, Views on One Day Cricket and the Award of a Benefit

The retirement of Reg Perks following just one season of captaincy brought Peter Richardson to the helm. A free scoring, elegant left-hander, he would play 34 Tests and average 37. In a cold, wet and unpleasant season, his task was to stop the rot after a dismal display in 1955.

Contrary to expectations the County proved a hard side to beat. While many games were drawn, including some from perilous looking positions, only four games were lost compared with eighteen during the previous season. With Kenyon as Richardson's opening partner, the pair aimed to ensure that Worcestershire could get off to the best possible start.

Vice-captain Roly Jenkins set out through sheer enthusiasm, to help improve the overall standard of play and he especially targeted the fielding. There was the arrival of Roy Booth behind the stumps, which, combined with the exuberance and brilliant close catching of Dick Richardson, meant that at least there was more purpose in the field.

The opening game was a stern test. The touring Australians threw everything at the home-side but could only manage a draw. The 10,000 spectators were treated to some hostile bowling from the visitors. For the third time, Ray Lindwall dismissed Don, this time lbw for 21, with Worcestershire subsiding to 90 all out. Brian Chapman, writing in the *Daily Mirror*, wrote, 'Never have I watched such a collection of unsentimental blokes as the cricketers who pounded and pulverised poor Worcestershire.' He also stated that he thought the Australian batting was going to be a tough nut to crack and continued, 'I've always cherished the memory of a ball Sonny Ramadhin once bowled at Lord's as the best I ever saw. The one that blinded Kenyon with lethal science today was of the same class. It was Lindwall's slower one. It swung in late; its length and flight were something the magician Merlin might have served up at the Round Table.'

In reply Australia amassed 438 all out, with George Chesterton (4 – 131) and Jack Flavell (4 – 115) claiming four wickets each. Chesterton got through 56 overs in taking his wickets.

The real entertainment came from Richie Benaud, who, batting at number seven, cracked 160 at a great rate of knots. It took him just 200 minutes to reach his score, which included 3 sixes and 22 fours. On the last day, a determined home-side batted all day and managed to hold out for a draw. This was thanks to Captain Peter Richardson's unbeaten 130, which batted him into contention for a place in the Test side.

Writing in the *Birmingham Mail* a few days later, Don went on record stating that

> Lindwall is still the Number One in the world. After having twice fallen victim to him in the match just ended at Worcester, I will willingly go on the stand to testify that Ray Lindwall is still the greatest bowler of his type in the world.
>
> Students of the game will probably have noticed a change in Ray's physique. He is at least two stones lighter than on his last visit. For the last year or more he's been on a reasonably strict diet, as a result of picking up a liver virus. He is now a complete tea-totaller which is quite contrary to the nature of most quick bowlers.

While a narrow defeat by just one wicket in the first Championship match was a disappointing start, Roly Jenkins took ten wickets in the game and three of the top six batsmen – including Don – scored fifties. This was backed up by a 123 run victory over neighbours Warwickshire and an 82 run victory over Somerset at Worcester. Don had scored three half-centuries and was in decent touch.

Three additional half-centuries came Don's way over the next eight games with just two victories and six draws. That said, the side was becoming harder to beat and was showing more determination in its play than it had in 1955. This was best demonstrated by Laddie Outschoorn who batted for over 6 hours scoring 154 not out to save the game against Hampshire at Cowes on the Isle of Wight. In this game Martin Horton weighed in with 70 in each innings to underline the promise he was showing.

Martin's best performance, however, was with the ball in the game against Somerset at Bath. Having been dismissed for just 113 in their first innings and 133 in their second, Worcestershire still won by 76 runs thanks to spells from Horton of 6 – 38 from 26 overs and 7 – 29 from 15 overs to dismiss the home-side for just 90 and 80 respectively.

Throughout the early weeks of the season, Don was not enjoying the best of luck. At Northampton he had to suffer some unpleasant knocks from Frank Tyson, especially a blow to the forearm which necessitated an X-ray; fortunately it revealed no damage. At Romford he had three days sickness due to a chill, through pain from a course of massage while he had also tripped up in the shower and damaged his ribs. However, the closest call was at Cowes when he fell from a 3 feet concrete terrace and crashed backwards into a brass balustrade, again with no lasting damage caused. As Don said, 'The luck is sure to turn some day!'

During this time Don continued to write for The *Birmingham Mail* in his regular slot. It's interesting to note two specific articles he wrote which demonstrated his understanding and forward thinking about the game. This knowledge of the game ultimately made him the very best of captains. His first concern was in respect of dwindling gates and expressed how disappointing and difficult he and the players found it to play in front of so few people. He went on to say,

> Already Worcestershire are experiencing an apathy towards the game. One would have thought that after we had beaten Warwickshire, the fans would have turned up to show their appreciation at the match which followed at New Road against

Somerset. But no, far from it. I can assure you that as a team we were all very disappointed to see how few members of the general public were interested to see if we could repeat the win against Somerset.

Stern words, but a sentiment which many Chief Executives would echo today, especially as attendances at Championship games can be very poor.

The second insight into Don's thinking appeared in another article when he posed the question 'will Sunday cricket have to come?' He wrote,

> One interesting proposal I read made a strong point that the number of county matches should be drastically cut down and that Sunday should be brought in as a full cricket day.
>
> The main argument in this case was that more amateurs could be brought into the game because if matches were played on Saturdays, Sundays and Mondays all they would need to do would be to get a long weekend off from their business commitments. Nor would I be opposed to cutting down the number of championship matches. What I do feel might need to come in is the one match per week lasting four days instead of three, if only to ensure that we get more outright results.
>
> It has been suggested that the rest of each week should be devoted to some kind of knockout competition, but I would be very wary about the idea. I think you know me well enough to appreciate that I like to get on with the scoring, but the knockout cricket is an artificial kind of game and no substitute for the real thing.

Opinion is still divided on both of these subjects to this day. Players and coaches make the point that they need more time in between games to rest and practice their skills, yet the demands placed upon them necessitate playing more and more cricket of varying duration to satisfy the needs of television, sponsors and the money makers in the game.

While some would say that the current approach of more short form cricket is designed to attract newer and younger audiences, those of a certain vintage argue that the roll on roll off nature of fixtures is to the detriment and integrity of the game.

It was not until 20 June that Don recorded his first three figure score of the season in the game against Cambridge University at Worcester. A first innings 112 from Laddie Outschoorn and 116 from Don in the second innings allowed acting captain Roly Jenkins (Peter Richardson was away on Test duty in the opening match at Trent Bridge) to set the students 245 to win in two and a half hours. They closed on 210 – 8 and had made a good fist of the run chase.

During this game Worcestershire handed a first class debut to Alf Tasker who came from Southwark, London. It was uneventful, however, as a lifelong collector of Worcestershire players' autographs, I traced Alf down to his home in Bentleigh, Victoria, Australia in 2001 and explained that I was in the process of obtaining the signature of every Worcestershire player to have played first class cricket since the War. To many people this might sound a strange pursuit for a grown man, but for some, you will identify the hook and recognise that once cricket gets into the bloodstream you are smitten for life. Tom Sears, the former Commercial Manager at New Road Worcester, once said to me, 'Tim, you need to get out more ... and I don't mean to watch more cricket.' That sums up beautifully the addictive nature of our much loved game.

Alf duly obliged, and in a revealing letter commented about a second game (not first class) just a few days after his debut, this time against the RAF:

In the RAF game I was initiated by the famous umpire Dai Davies. I was keeping wicket and he would pretend the over was completed after only five balls. He would walk away from the bowler's end whereupon he would return to his post having a great laugh at my expense and to the amusement of my fellow players. He did this to me on two occasions.

On the final day of this match, Worcestershire were in trouble and I came out to bat in the lower order and Umpire Davies remarked in a loud voice to the opposition that he was pleased that the game would soon be over as he would now be able to catch the early train home. I then proceeded to bat for two hours for 20.

Raman Subba Row tried bowling donkey drops to encourage me to hit out, but I just put the dead bat on them. It was not pretty to watch but I was determined that Mr Davies would miss his train. Forty-five years later, I still get a chuckle out of that incident.

The drawn game at Swansea proved profitable with Don scoring his second century in two games. *The South Wales Echo's* headline read: 'Glamorgan Men Fail to Pin Down Worcester'. Kenyon, who had looked supremely confident throughout the innings, reached his century in three hours and fifty minutes and included 17 fours. In total he batted for just under six hours for a total of 171 containing 1 six and 27 fours and was ultimately bowled by Don Shepherd.

The *Sports Argus* was less sympathetic with its headline; 'Kenyon hammers leeks into Glamorgan field.' – 'Dashing Don Kenyon knows how to take advantage of his luck. With Glamorgan fielders dropping catches all over the field at Swansea, the Worcestershire opener chanced his arm and was rewarded with a second century in two days.'

It proved to be a record that wasn't. Over the loudspeakers at the ground it announced that Don had beaten 'Doc' Gibbons' record of having scored the most hundreds for Worcestershire. Kenyon's was his forty-third and Gibbons was stated to have scored forty-two. *Wisden*, however, correctly stated that Gibbons had scored forty-four first class hundreds, something which is verified in Les Hatton's *100 Greats of Worcestershire County Cricket Club*. In early May 2014 I spoke with Don Shepherd the man who dismissed him, he had very vivid recollection of the game:

The first time I saw Don was at Kiddy [Kidderminster] in 1950. It rained and rained, we only had nine hours play but we were just happy to be there. I was happy because I got him out for 9. I judge openers by their attitude as well as skill. For some, if it doesn't happen in the first hour, you knew you were in for a long day. Don was one of those. At the time New Road was a pearler of a pitch and he got runs by the thousand ... 2,000 of them in 1950.

He always had a wry smile, as if he was enjoying the job he was paid to do. He was very strong off his legs and off middle stump once he was in because if he stayed in, he'd score heavily. A quiet bloke, I didn't get to know him off the field really well but respected him hugely; if there was one word to sum him up it would be reliable – as good a way as any to sum him up.

I do remember 1956 well, it was his forty-third century and I got him out, but not before he had scored 171.

At this point Don Shepherd was laughing loudly at his own misfortune. It was good to have spent a few moments enjoying the reminiscences of a true great of Glamorgan cricket and a really decent bloke to boot.

Worcestershire were to embark on a winning streak of three consecutive games, and during the one against Gloucestershire Don passed his 1,000 runs for the season. In the last of the trio of games he was at his very best when Yorkshire visited Kidderminster in the second week of July.

Batting first, Don reached his hundred in four hours and went on to complete his double hundred in just a further 119 minutes. Overnight he was 218 and was finally dismissed for 259. This innings, which contained a six and 31 fours, was the highest score of his career, it also meant that Worcestershire could declare at 440 – 6. Even so, the papers next day were asking only one key question: Could Don force his way back into the England side? *The Birmingham Gazette* stated,

> Kenyon's form raises the pertinent question of whether we shall see two Worcestershire openers playing for England. A few more days like yesterday and Kenyon must surely come under consideration as an in-form batsman. True, the wicket gave no help at all to the bowlers but the Yorkshire attack was more like tepid tea than the sparkling champagne offensive when Fearless Freddie is present.

Yorkshire were dismissed for 163 (Bob Berry 5 – 49) and 183 (Martin Horton 5 – 64) meaning they subsided to an innings and 94 run defeat, which was the first time Worcestershire had beaten the white-rose county by an innings margin.

The inability to put a run of victories together was evidenced by three consecutive drawn games, the sequence being broken in the victory against Derbyshire at Dudley and what a performance it turned out to be.

Batting first Worcestershire opened up with 384 – 4 declared. John Davis in the *Birmingham Gazette* wrote, 'In a five and a half hour onslaught, they pounded third in the table Derbyshire. Don Kenyon once more gave notice that he is a force to be reckoned with. His 147 was made in an innings notable also for the complete absence of a faulty stroke and put him first in the race to 2,000 runs.'

Kenyon's runs were scored at over a run a minute which contained 23 fours; it was Don at his devastating best. This was his 45th career hundred, had now passed Doc Gibbons' county record following the false start during the game at Swansea. Worcestershire's opening bowler that day was a very quick, John Aldridge who claimed 3 – 45 and 2 – 37 in the game and recalls what Don was like as a person:

I found him a very amicable man, he was lovely. One thing he taught me in life has always stayed with me. I asked him one day why he never hooked. His reply, 'John, know your capabilities.' Throughout life I remember this ... know your capabilities.

He used to pick me up with George Dews and Jack Flav (Jack Flavell) when I lived in Hartlebury. That's when I played in the first team, because if you were not selected, you had to make your own way there.

Derbyshire were dismissed for 228 with Roly Jenkins the hero of the bowling attack with 5 – 62 from 25 overs in the first innings and 6 – 50 from 18 overs in the second. It meant Worcestershire triumphed by ten wickets inside two days. Sadly for Roly, he went from hero to zero when Yorkshire gained revenge for the defeat at Kidderminster by inflicting a ten wicket defeat on the visitors at Bradford. For the only time in a twenty-one-year career, Roly bagged a pair, Raymond Illingworth and Johnny Wardle being the successful bowlers.

Just one victory was achieved from the remaining fixtures, a 65 run winning margin over Glamorgan at Worcester. Don finished the season with 1,994 first class runs at 40.69 to underline another fine season as the side climbed to a more respectable ninth position. We can't leave 1956 without noting that Don even had a taste of bowling, though it was only a two over spell in the game at Essex.

It was the first time in seven seasons that he had 'failed' to reach 2,000 runs. If the remainder of the last game against Surrey had not been washed out and the England XI against a Commonwealth XI at Torquay not been abandoned without a ball being bowled, he would surely have achieved it. Any disappointment Don may have felt for not reaching 2,000 runs was short lived, though, because the news followed that he had been awarded a benefit in 1957.

A winter of planning lay ahead.

Chapter 10

Benefit Season and Beyond

Writing for the *Evening Despatch* in January 1957, Dick Knight appealed to the people of the Black Country to get behind Don Kenyon's benefit and described him as 'one of the country's most consistent run getters for seasons.'

Long-time friend Norman Whiting was determined to do something to recognise Don and instigated a knock-out competition with thirty-two clubs taking part. The early rounds were to consist of evening matches, each innings being of fifteen 8-ball overs. The final was scheduled to be played at Stourbridge CC on a Sunday with Don present, and all the proceeds were for his benefit. The aim of the competition was to continue in subsequent years for other worthy cricket causes.

Terry Church, in his book *Lost Cricket and Football Clubs and Grounds in the South of the Black Country*, describes the competition in more detail:

> The competition attracted entries from clubs of contrasting strengths varying from Birmingham League clubs to village sides, although the former category tended to dominate. It was probably the foremost competition of its kind in the West Midlands.
>
> In the mid-1970s the competition committee changed the format of the then twenty-over competition with the final being played on a two-leg basis at the ground of each finalist, the result being decided over the two games. The patron of the competition, Don Kenyon, presented the trophies and individual medals at a presentation evening and dance held at The Old White Horse in Stourbridge.

Sadly, with the onset of more and more midweek leagues emerging, the competition went into decline and folded in the late 1980s.

In 1957 the Worcestershire side was led once more by Peter Richardson who, understandably after three full seasons and two strenuous tours, was showing signs of tiredness during the season when playing for the County. Internationally, though, he had a successful summer and scored centuries at Nottingham and The Oval for England against the West Indies and averaged 58.71.

Worcestershire seemed to lack any sense of purpose which was underlined in the fielding, which regressed sharply from the encouragement of the year before. Unfortunately the season was all too disappointing and the team fell to sixteenth in the table, the lowest position since 1934. The art of bowling also deserted Roly Jenkins completely. He struggled to maintain length, flight and control and although typically he spent hours in the nets trying to find a solution, he managed just twenty-nine wickets all season. The only bowler to come out of the season with any credibility was Jack Flavell, who claimed 100 wickets.

The batting was criticised and although the batsmen were capable of quick scoring, they did not do so often enough in the first innings. As a result fourteen games were drawn, four won and nine lost. Perversely, six batsmen passed a 1,000 runs and Don once more was at the front of the queue.

In April a protest was registered against an early season benefit game for Don, between Rugeley Cricket Club and a Don Kenyon All-Star team. With 5,000 tickets printed and sold, the objection was raised by one of Rugeley's players, a vicar by the name of Reverend Ronald Cason, a good club cricketer himself. Although scheduled for a Sunday, the organisers overlooked the fact that 21 April was Easter Sunday. With the protest duly noted, the game went ahead; a minor crisis had been averted.

In early May, the West Indian tourists stopped off in Worcester for the traditional opener to the season. The visitors only managed 290 all out with Bob Berry claiming 6 – 106 from his 44 overs. Disastrously, Worcestershire were dismissed for 89 in just 32 overs and following on subsided to 133 all out. The main destroyer was Denis Atkinson who returned figures of 5 – 25 and 5 – 37. Don had the dubious honour of being out twice before lunch on the same day! Garry Sobers stole the show in the second innings with a miraculous horizontal catch at fine leg just inches off the ground.

Meanwhile Don's second innings of the championship yielded 88 runs in the drawn game with Warwickshire at Dudley. On the rest day another benefit game was arranged, this one at the Accles and Pollock ground in Oldbury with Don putting out pretty much a full strength Worcestershire side.

His shrewd judgement of the game was clearly evident in his customary article for the *Birmingham Mail* on Saturday 14 May when he suggested that changes to the laws of the game would leave 'some very disappointed bowlers'. He went on to explain, 'The restriction on the number of fielders on the leg side behind the wicket is going to penalise some bowlers more than others, we must equally be mindful that the law also says that not more than five fielders must be used on the whole of the leg side.' Being forthright as ever in his views on the game he commented further, 'Personally I don't really take kindly to any suggestion which aims at dictating to a skipper where and how he must place his field but since it has been accepted that is how the counties will have to play the game – at least for 1957.'

There appears to be a tongue in cheek acceptance of the changes, but almost an air of 'told you so' that the law is bound to change again the following season.

One might argue that the game has always been tinkered with. In the mid-1970s I was personally disappointed when the fast bowlers' secret weapon, the bouncer, was restricted. It took away an air of excitement from the game and with other restrictions such as prescriptive field placing in the one day format becoming more and more prevalent, one can argue that the contests are becoming easier to predict, in danger of boring the spectator.

Don's first century of the season came in a thriller against Gloucestershire at Bristol. In reply to the home-side's 307, Worcestershire compiled 313 – 9 declared, thanks to a two hours 40 minutes 115 from Don, which included 12 fours. Dick Richardson weighed in with 101 not out and was fast becoming the 'star of the future' if the newspapers were to be believed.

Thanks to Tom Graveney's 111 not out in Gloucestershire's second knock, an innings likened to the style of a 'beautiful liner' in Worcestershire's Club Yearbook for 1958, Worcestershire were set 218 to win. Not to be out done, Peter Richardson scored the fastest hundred of the game (108) in just one hour forty-three minutes to help steer Worcestershire to their first win of the season by five wickets and with just 12 minutes of the game to spare.

The form of the Richardson brothers was to earn them both Test appearances during the summer, and at Trent Bridge in the Third Test, they found themselves in the same side for Dick's Test debut. More light entertainment was available at the end of May in another benefit game. Smethwick Drop Forgings Ltd organised it at their Stourport Road ground where a Worcestershire team took on fifteen players from the Kidderminster district.

The *Kidderminster Shuttle* reported, 'Don Kenyon the Worcestershire and England opening batsman delighted the big crowd by hitting a splendid century, 117 out of a total of 164 – 7 declared. His innings contained 3 sixes and 15 fours.' Don even had a rare bowl and finished with two wickets from just five balls, all of which contributed £186 2s 3d to his fund.

A second first class century of the season came in the game against Oxford University at The Parks, his 119 in the second innings allowing Worcestershire to win by 178 runs. Don's innings was described in the 1958 County Yearbook, 'He really got into gear and scored his runs with the greatest of ease in two hours ten minutes, hitting 18 fours.' This was a welcome return to some sort of form; he had been nowhere near his best up to this point of the season.

The other pleasing aspect of the game at Oxford was the form of Len Coldwell, who returned figures of 6 – 30 from 16 overs and 5 – 18 from 19 overs. Ten days later, Derbyshire were on the receiving end during the game at Derby.

Don opening with Peter Richardson, the pair put on 175 for the first wicket at a rate of 70 an hour which was described by George Stokes in the *Birmingham Mail*:

> Worcestershire pasted the Derbyshire bowling to such an extent that in 260 minutes batting up to tea they had put on 296 runs, including centuries from each of their openers and had only lost three wickets.
>
> Peter Richardson had the distinction of getting his century before lunch and finished with 116 out of 175. Richardson positively raced away with a dazzling array of strokes, glances, cover drives, straight drives, and pulls, all along the carpet.

Although the visitors declared on 403 – 7, and despite of Don's 175, it was insufficient to force a win, Derbyshire closing their second innings on 228 – 8, batting out time to save the game. The next game at New Road was against Combined Services, which saw Don score a 50 in each innings. I had an insight into this game thanks to accessing a rare homemade video shot by former Worcestershire player Derek Pearson who recorded a conversation he had with

Don during the Worcestershire Old Players Association reunion in 1993.

> Don: I was directed to play against Combined Services in 1957 just to assess your ability. They were all worried about that … [cocking his wrist as a bowler would to deliver the ball] you know what I'm on about Derek? [This was an indirect reference to Derek's action for which he was called for throwing just two years later]
> Derek: Do you remember how you were out? [A shake of head followed]
> Derek: I hit you in the midriff and you were given out lbw. [This was very amusing to both of them, Don was obviously enjoying being reminded by Derek]
> Derek: The captain was A. C. Shirreff, one of the nicest men you could meet, who went on to coach Somerset.
> Don: He was captain when I played for Combined Services in 1946 against Cambridge at Fenner's. I went in first and got a ton but J. G. W. Davies, himself an academic and fine cricketer who played for Kent, said that I'd had enough batting and ran me out. As a twenty-two-year-old I told myself that would never happen again and it didn't.

It was quite evident to see from the look on Don's face that he meant it nearly fifty years after the event. This proved yet again, how driven he was and that his cricket was not to be taken lightly.

At the end of June 1957 Don hit a purple patch by first scoring 123 in the first innings against Sussex at Eastbourne, an innings which contained seventeen fours and was described as 'standing head and shoulders above anyone else'. The game ended with the scores level, but due to the complex nature of the points scoring system, Worcestershire collected six points as the side batting fourth in a drawn game which ends with the scores level! The allocation of bonus points in today's game is much easier to understand, trust me!

Overnight the team had to travel to start a game against Nottinghamshire at Worcester the following day, but Don showed great tenacity in Worcestershire's first innings. In reply to Nottinghamshire's 265, the home-side declared on 292 – 6 with Don 200 not out. George Stokes, writing in the *Birmingham Mail*, said,

> It was a remarkable performance to score 200 not out in a total of 292, especially when one considers the strain of having to play with extreme caution for the whole of six hours at the wicket.
>
> It would have gone ill with the side had his wicket fallen, for five of the six men who had been dismissed up to that point had scored only sixteen runs between them.

This had been Don at his best because when he reached 154 he became, at the age of thirty-three years and fifty days, the youngest Worcestershire player to reach 20,000 first class runs, a record which stood until Graeme Hick passed it in 1998.

I asked Graeme in 2013 whether he had ever met or talked to Don, something he might have done when Don was Worcestershire President between 1986 and 1989. He replied, 'I don't know much about him to be honest, but I do know what he did for Worcestershire, you just have to look around the place. From the little I had to do with him, I just remember him as being a lovely gentleman.'

The benefit year continued apace with a range of functions, one noteworthy event being the opening of the pavilion at Oldswinford Cricket Club near Stourbridge in the West Midlands.

Don was friendly for many years with Jack Edmonds from Oldswinford CC and, according to Jean Kenyon, they would go and have a pint most evenings. She said that Don used to like to encourage the local team and would attend presentations, awards and social evenings by way of support.

It was not until the last week of August that Don recorded another hundred but, in the period between the game at Eastbourne in June up until the end of August, only one win was recorded, with eight draws and five defeats which made for a poor return. One match of significance, however, was the game against Gloucestershire starting on 20 July at New Road; it was Don's benefit match. Sadly the weather ruined the first day's play on the Saturday, thus reducing the chance of a result in the game. With honours even on first innings, Worcestershire closed day three on 151 – 6, the highlights of the ruined game being half-centuries from Dick Richardson in the first innings (60) and Bob Broadbent (60 not out) in the second.

Don's final century of the season came in the game against Sussex at New Road in the last week of August but it was yet another drawn game. Hundreds in the Sussex first innings from Ken Suttle and Jim Parks were balanced out by 119 from Don who according to the Club's 1958 Yearbook, 'gave a fine display.'

A second hundred in the game from Jim Parks left Worcestershire little time to chase the 193 for victory, but once again, rain had interfered with the game. Despite the volume of runs, Jack Flavell finished with match figures of 11 – 155 to further enhance his reputation and to justify his status as bowler of the season.

The final act of the season was for Don to play in two games at the Torquay Festival in early September. He represented the England XI (scores of 13 and 42) which drew with a Commonwealth XI and was in the North team (scores of 9 and 7) which was defeated by the South. Both teams were packed with good cricketers: Raymond Illingworth, Jack Robertson, George Emmett, Charles Palmer, Fred Titmus and Keith Andrew turned out for the England XI, with Roy Marshall, Bill Alley, Colin McCool and Peter Wight all turning out for the Commonwealth XI.

The season closed with Don scoring 2,231 first class and 1,847 championship runs with six centuries. It's interesting to note the comment in the 1958 Worcestershire Club Yearbook when it reported that 'one is forced to wonder whether the organisation of a benefit is good for a man's cricket?' Although Don's form in the latter part of the season had been indifferent, many players would be content with his return for a season's work; but the decline in the team's performance was probably more of a concern.

At the start of 1958 Don's benefit figure was announced, a Worcestershire record at the time of £3,840 . While the social events were a thing of the past, three former players all commented to me about Don and how he was perceived in a social setting. All are revealing in different ways. Alan Ormrod said,

> Don would socialise when he wanted to – but he had to be ready to do it. He was
> not a joke teller, he would laugh at others but was a serious man. He came from

With Peter Richardson in 1957 opening the Oldswinford CC Pavilion. From the Kenyon family collection.

Torquay Cricket Festival, 1957. From the Kenyon family collection.

war time when things were hard and everyone was recovering. His philosophy was that he needed to make everything secure.

I never really got to know him truly well. He rarely let his hair down which meant you didn't get to know him as you'd like to know him. He helped you in how to conduct your life, how to play cricket and be a decent person. That is the way he lived his life and was an example to us all. He held no grudges about anyone, but if you didn't listen to him you were an idiot.

Former Worcestershire player and subsequent chairman, John Elliott contributed:

In the early days as I got to know him he was never a drinking man but for the last three or four years, until I left in 1965, he liked a drink; he was a changed man. From being teatotal he got stuck in and enjoyed the fun of life, maybe that was because he was getting close to the end of his career? He could be tight, if you went to a function he'd fill his boots with food and drink ... and the free cigarettes.

Norman Whiting stated:

The trouble in cricket is if you get a captain who fills his team with pals. They like to socialise and go horseracing together, but not Don; he was very much a one off. At night, I'd go out with George Dews and Bob Broadbent but Don would go out, on what he called, 'window shopping' so that he didn't have to spend a great deal.

I think this is the reason for his not being a great Test player; he didn't mix well in that environment. On the tour to India in 51 – 52, five or six would be having a drink and he'd be in the corner reading a book. He'd say, 'I'm not going in here buying six drinks because I won't get six back.

He was a real loner in that respect, he didn't want to waste money. He didn't start with much and his ambition was to make a good living, that's all he wanted. Yes, he was very much his own man.

Don was now in a position to turn his attention to the new season and in the opening game of 1958 New Zealand were the visitors. Peter Richardson won the toss and made first use of the pitch, with the top six all getting a start the captain himself registering 104 out of a total of 345 – 7 declared. Don's contribution was 43. In the visitors' total of 283 all out, Bert Sutcliffe weighed in with 139 before being stumped by Roy Booth off Roly Jenkins. His innings which lasted five and a half hours contained 21 fours.

Worcestershire declared their second innings on 202 – 4 with Don unbeaten on 102 which included 17 fours and had taken a shade over three hours to compile. The visitors, set 264 to win, reached 202 – 8 by the close and at one point were in danger of being bowled out thanks to 4 – 59 from Roly Jenkins and 3 – 50 from Martin Horton.

The early exchanges of the season saw Worcestershire win just one championship match from the first four, however, the bowling was showing signs of improvement with Derek Pearson (5 – 38 in the victory over Gloucestershire) and Jack Flavell (6 – 47 in the draw with Hampshire) showing good form.

On the way to 43 vs New Zealand at New Road in 1958. From the Kenyon family collection.

In the game at Romford against Essex, Don sustained an injury which was to keep him out for the next five games. Writing his regular column for the *Birmingham Mail*, he was in philosophical mood about it,

> What is the batsman's most vulnerable spot when he is at the wicket? No doubt about it – it's the thumb of the right hand of a right handed player and of the left hand of a left-hander. I found that out to my cost when we played Essex at Romford when I chipped a bone in my right thumb. I realise that I have been lucky in the matter of injuries for this was my first serious knock in twelve years as a professional batsman.

Laddie Outschoorn was moved back to open in Don's absence but Don returned for the game against Leicester at Worcester on 18 June. The Club's 1959 Yearbook firmly expressed its opinion: 'Kenyon was lacking confidence for some matches to follow which was very unfortunate after such a good start to the season.'

Indeed, the next six games yielded Don just 250 runs from twelve innings and with the season entering the third week of July a first championship hundred of the campaign hadn't yet materialised. On a brighter note, during that run of six games, the County had won three, drawn one and lost just the two games.

Thankfully the visit of Gloucestershire provided a welcome return to some sort of form for him with 94 in the first innings and 79 in the second, the knocks contributing to a win by 88 runs. A five wicket haul in the first innings from John Aldridge (5 – 45) was the highlight of the bowling effort.

The relief was evident from the headline in the *Sports News*: 'Hooray! Don's

Back among the Runs' while the *Express and Star*'s headline read: 'Polished 94 by Don Kenyon'. It went on to state: 'On a perfect pitch and a fast outfield the Gloucestershire bowlers toiled with little reward, while Worcestershire, thanks to a scintillating start by Peter Richardson and Don Kenyon, amassed 332. In a bright three and a half hours Kenyon scored 94 including thirteen boundaries, his best score since the opening match of the season.'

Ten days later Don recorded his first and only championship century of the season, 107 in the second innings of the game against Hampshire at New Road. With Martin Horton weighing in with 133 Worcestershire were able to save the game against the table-topping visitors. As Don reached 60 he passed the 1,000 run mark for the season, but it proved an uphill battle for him compared with previous seasons.

In early August Don missed two more matches against Northants and Middlesex due to a broken finger, adding to the frustration of a stop, start season for him. Just one more half-century capped off a miserable season with just 1,438 runs in all first class matches and only the two centuries to his name. At least the final game against Champions Surrey at The Oval had proved a thrilling encounter thanks mainly to a first innings 117 from Martin Horton out of a total of 230 by the visitors.

At 110 – 2 Alec Bedser surprisingly declared Surrey's first innings, so Worcestershire responded by declaring their second innings at 54 – 5 to leave Surrey 175 to win. Jack Flavell with 4 – 23 and Martin Horton (3 – 19) destroyed Surrey who were dismissed for 57, which was the first time since they first met in 1900 that Worcestershire had dismissed them for under 100. It also meant that Jack Flavell had taken 100 wickets for the season. A more creditable position of ninth in the Championship gave hope of a brighter future. 1958 had also brought the retirement of Roly Jenkins one of Worcestershire's most colourful cricketers. In a twenty year career he took 1,148 wickets at just 23.72 apiece and was a cricketer of great energy and humour both on and off the field.

After retiring, he bought a sweet shop in Worcester where it was reported that he would buy the *Financial Times* – because he had invested a sum of money – but Don would read it to prevent him having to buy a copy. Don was ever the shrewd one when it came to money matters!

Chapter 11

The New Captain and Dealing with an Immediate Crisis

As the players prepared for the first match scheduled for 29 April 1959, shock news surfaced on Friday 17th. Unexpectedly, Peter Richardson had stood down as captain amidst a flurry of speculation. Some cited personal reasons while others hinted that he had approached the club during the summer of 1958 with a request to turn professional. He had even been linked with the captaincy of Glamorgan. He had returned from the MCC tour of Australia a week earlier, but had not reported back with the Worcestershire players for practice and had not been seen at the ground.

The *Express and Star* ran the headline: 'Richardson's Future in the Balance' and reported, 'Mr J. Lister, County Secretary, said today Peter Richardson had written asking the committee not to consider him for the captaincy and had intimated it was unlikely he would be available to play for the side.' The request from Peter Richardson was considered and approved by the committee but they said they were firmly of the opinion he should continue to play for the County. In the *Express and Star* Peter commented, 'I don't know whether I shall remain in cricket. A lot depends on whether I am asked. Obviously I should like to continue to play, but no other county have made a definite approach to me.'

The committee decided there was one man with the experience and knowledge to step into the Captain's breach, and that man was thirty-four year old Don Kenyon. With the change of Captain, came a change of Secretary, Richardson had held both positions, so Joe Lister who had shared that role with him hastily took over as sole incumbent but the controversy rumbled on.

The *Birmingham Mail*, Friday 17 April, reported that Richardson was definitely not sacked and that Worcestershire intended to reappoint him to the playing staff. Richardson, on the other hand, said he did not want to be considered. The committee was holding firm too and stated, 'We are firmly of the opinion that he should continue to play for the County.' As it transpired, Peter Richardson had played his last match for Worcestershire, so Don was left to pick up the pieces. With typical diplomacy he said, 'I am very pleased at the appointment. I shall make no personal approach to Peter, but if he is going to be available I shall be happy to have him in the side. As far as I'm concerned Peter is still a very good friend and only hope he stays in cricket. I don't know the reasons for him making the decision any more than anyone else.' It was now time for some serious net practice ahead of the first game against India.

It was not long into the match that Don had to deal with his first crisis. The very quick Derek Pearson was no-balled for throwing by the much respected umpire and former Worcestershire wicketkeeper, Syd Buller. In November 2013 I spent a fantastic evening in Derek's company reminiscing about his time at Worcester and in particular Don's response to the handling of the no-ball affair. Derek recalled,

> Don was a very private man. I thought if you want someone who knows the game inside out and backwards, he was the man who was best to lead the team. He was not the sort of person to pursue people if you needed him to rattle cages that was not his style.
>
> Like Tom Graveney and P. B. H. May they all had the same perfection in terms of style. If you have a perfect style, as a batsman you can play for a long time. If early or late you can still hit through the line, however, if you cross bat, your timing has to be perfect. [Derek leant forward in his chair and played the most exquisite cover drive in the Kenyon mould and smiled] That's the way he used to play it, perfect.
>
> In the winter of '58 we took a good team to Australia but Gordon Rorke and Ian Meckiff were accused of throwing by our players who said they were quick. I'm told third hand that the authorities were due to have a worldwide conference to decide who threw – I was on the list. Unbeknown to anyone, they were on my case as early as 1959 but nobody had mentioned it to Don or the club. I had previously been no-balled in the early 1950s and was sent to Alf Gover's school where they were satisfied but slow motion does now show how some people throw!
>
> When they arrived at New Road they were after anyone with a suspicious action. Apparently the MCC decided they would clandestinely film bowlers and someone was given the job of dishing out the cameras. Suddenly players would see someone appear from behind the sight screen for no apparent reason and this went on for several years. I guess I must be on film but cannot find anything in the archive, sadly it was broken up. I did track down the man who filmed it, but he told me I wasn't ultimately in it because I had been no-balled and was no longer a suspect. Therefore, there is no film.
>
> Don's response to Syd Buller calling me was done in the usual way. He was very nice, in no way irate just calm but you didn't know what was going on underneath like so many calm people. He responded by doing the most practical thing and that was to send me to Syd's end so he couldn't see me and therefore, no longer no-ball me. That was the measure of Don, a no frills captain, he did it his way if he believed he was right. The game could then move on without fuss.
>
> Charlie Griffith and I were regarded as the two fastest bowlers in the world at the time. Keith Miller, who reported on the game, was quoted as saying, 'This boy does not throw, that's a good enough endorsement for me.' Syd Buller was an honest person and a much respected umpire, he did what he thought was right. There was never an evil intention; however, he wouldn't talk about it, not wanting to compromise his impartiality.

Although Derek finished with 4 – 40, the game ended in a draw with Bob Broadbent (102 not out) and George Dews (122) batting the visitors out of the game with a total of 305 in response to their 219.

Worcestershire lost their opening Championship game at Swansea where, for all money, it looked like they would win. A brilliant second innings 89 from Dews, who combated the threat of Jim McConnon (8 – 62) helped steer Worcestershire to a lead of 262. Gilbert Parkhouse (111) and Bernard Hedges (79) put on 170 for the first wicket with Glamorgan then cruising home by six wickets.

Three defeats in the next four games was a disappointing return for the new captain. His first win came in a seven wicket victory over Gloucestershire at Stroud at the end of May. 126 from Dick Richardson in the first innings and Jack Flavell with 5 – 116 in Gloucestershire's second innings were the main contributors to the Worcester effort. Horton continued his prime form with 161 against Cambridge University in the next match described as 'a boring game which ended in a tame draw!'

Don's indifferent form continued, at the Oval his good friend Alec Bedser claimed 6 – 46 including the wicket of Don, to steer Surrey to a comfortable nine wicket victory. The breakthrough hundred came in the next game when, despite it ending in one of the season's many draws, Don (107) put on 202 for the first wicket with Laddie Outschoorn (103) against Nottinghamshire at Worcester. The *Sports News* referred to the innings as a 'welcome return to form for Kenyon' and as the innings progressed reported 'conditions were anything but pleasant, but Kenyon and Outschoorn were not worried by the weather on this batting paradise.'

The partnership had significant consequences because as the *Birmingham Mail* reported: 'They nearly missed the £500 boat!' A purse of £500 was on offer this season for the fastest 200 in the first innings of any match in an attempt to brighten up the opening stages of championship matches. It nearly didn't happen because the two batsmen were under the impression that they could not beat the best which had been previously set by Hampshire and eased off as a result. Members of the crowd were getting restless because they knew the true facts that the record was still on and managed to get a message out to the middle via the twelfth man. It had the desired effect because a sudden burst of renewed activity meant they got there with seven balls to spare.

It's not known what happened to the prize money, it was designed as a team prize so one can only assume in the interests of fair play it was put to that use.

A lean spell for both the team and Don followed. In six innings he could only muster 24 runs, during which time there were some notable performances by other individuals. John Aldridge claimed 7 – 104 in the game against Middlesex at Lord's while at Hove, Laddie Outschoorn hit 118, wicketkeeper Roy Booth struck a very polished 113 and Derek Pearson was at his best with 6 - 92. The efforts of Aldridge and Pearson were soon to be recognised.

Don bounced back from this minor slump with 229 in the first innings of the drawn game against Hampshire at Portsmouth. The report described it by stating, 'If Worcestershire's fielding was not all it might have been, the batting of their captain Kenyon was all that the big crowd could ask for to end a perfect day in the sun. He hit 19 off the first 2 overs and never lost his stride reaching his 50 in 50 minutes out of 67.'

John Aldridge described this as one of the best knocks he ever saw Don play; he recalled how hard he always struck the ball. Once again, John and Derek

Pearson were the pick of the bowlers in this game with four wickets apiece.

In the following game against Kent at New Road, Len Coldwell was the star of the show, with 8 – 55 and 3 – 70 in another drawn game in which a second innings 107 not out from Stuart Leary was enough to save Kent. In my conversation with Derek, he recalled what a lovely man Stuart was and how saddened he had been in 1988 to hear that he had taken his own life. The form of these three young quick bowlers earned them their county caps. Don, as captain, presented these to them, 'A very proud moment,' as Derek recalls. Ironically, John was no-balled for throwing only a few matches later in the game against Leicestershire at Kidderminster.

John Aldridge said,

> The umpire yet again was Syd Buller. We went to Accles and Pollock the next day to play a benefit game; I sat and talked to Frank Lee who had umpired the day before when I was called about it. The problem is 'when you bowl your bouncer' was all Frank said.
>
> I played in Australia where the umpire 'Col' Egar, who had called Ian Meckiff, watched me all day and said all you do is flick your wrist which suggested to me I was releasing the ball correctly. I asked Alec Bedser how he bowled his leg cutter; he showed me, put his middle finger around the seam and clicked his wrist back. That's how he did it and how I liked to do it.

Presentation of county caps to John Aldridge, Derek Pearson and Len Coldwell. From Derek Pearson's collection.

On the way to 63 against Essex at Leyton in 1959. The keeper is Brian Taylor and Tom Spencer the square leg umpire. From the Kenyon family collection.

Three more draws and a win at Leicester were at best an average return, Don's form again dipped in that period. Nonetheless, he made amends as usual when Leicestershire visited Kidderminster in mid-July.

A first innings duck and some indifferent batting meant that Worcestershire only mustered 162 all out. Four wickets from both the in-form John Aldridge and Martin Horton, who were described as virtually unplayable, restricted the visitors to 98 all out. Batting again, Don and Laddie Outschoorn put on 107 in 108 minutes for the first wicket with Don ultimately completing his ton before being out for 101.

The Club's 1960 Yearbook indicated that 'Kenyon looked in majestic form', his runs resulting in a declaration at 256 – 8. Leicestershire were dismissed for 128 with Martin Horton once more claiming 4 – 45 on what was described as a 'badly damaged wicket.' Over the next five weeks only one more win was recorded, a 135 run victory against Surrey with two defeats and yet more drawn games; six of them. The winds of change were evident because Don instigated some changes to the batting line up. Martin Horton was given the chance to open, with Don dropping to number four, a very rare occurrence for him, and Outschoorn and Ron Headley alternated as Martin's opening partner. Headley had deserved his chance, scoring 631 runs at 39.44 in the second XI underlining the potential everyone knew he had.

The move for Martin also paid dividends. In the second innings against Essex at Leyton he cracked 212, his first double hundred, and with George Dews (130) helped Worcestershire to 493 to save the game. The visitors had been over 200 behind on first innings, and during the rear-guard action, the Essex captain even resorted to giving all of his ten out fielders a bowl in an attempt to engineer a win.

These subtle changes were evidence of Don's ability to spot an opening and exploit it, but equally demonstrated his ability as a shrewd judge of a player.

Another Martin Horton century (106) plus 5 – 42 from Jack Flavell and 5 – 54 in the second innings from newcomer David Pratt, helped Worcestershire to a 135 run victory over Surrey at Worcester. As the season began to reach its climax in August, Don had a new lease of life with a match saving 125 in the second innings against Lancashire who were playing their first ever game at Southport. Behind by over 200 on first innings Don's effort helped avert defeat with the game finishing as a draw. This in effect put paid to any chance Lancashire had of winning the title.

1959 was fast becoming one of the most exciting seasons for many years. Right to the end of the season the result was so much in doubt that any one of six sides could have won the County Championship. Three of these sides were actually in the lead one after the other in late August with Surrey, Yorkshire and Gloucestershire all playing Worcestershire at critical times. Their victories against Surrey and ultimately Gloucestershire went some way to determine the outcome.

The penultimate game against Yorkshire at New Road did in effect help settle the Championship, a six wicket defeat handing the visitors the initiative. Despite 6 – 66 from Len Coldwell, Worcestershire were 142 behind on first innings and batting once more to save the game. W. R. Chignell's *History of Worcestershire CCC*, describes the closing exchanges of the game:

> The really grand batting came from Kenyon who played probably the best innings of the season at Worcester. While he was there, Yorkshire looked like anything but eventual champions. He scored 122 in 200 minutes and when he left, Worcestershire were 274 – 4, but they came back in typical Yorkshire style and Worcestershire were chased out for 301. This left Yorkshire with 160 to win in 158 minutes. At 87 – 4 the issue was in doubt, but shortly after Illingworth was dropped off a skier by Kenyon, he and Bolus brought Yorkshire safely home by six wickets.

The season concluded with an 83 run victory over Gloucestershire at Worcester with John Aldridge claiming another haul, (6 – 33 from 20 overs) and Don's first season as captain drew to a close. Personally he had scored 1,613 runs at 28.80 with five centuries but collectively the team had slipped to fourteenth in the table.

Despite this setback, there were signs of improvement which the captain could be pleased with. Seven batsmen scored 1,000 runs and although Jack Flavell was the only bowler to claim a hundred wickets, Horton, Coldwell, Pearson and Aldridge had taken well over fifty.

Chapter 12

The Signs are There

1959 had been a season of transition both on and off the pitch. The new season was eagerly anticipated and on New Year's Day 1960, cartoonist Norman Edwards of the *Evening Despatch* sketched his hope of optimism for the upcoming season with the 'Grand Kenyon' being at the forefront.

The finances of the club though were under scrutiny at the start of the season with the need for more income to be generated against a backcloth of dwindling attendances. The committee went to great lengths to promote the need for attacking and positive cricket. Many of today's chief executives, including Worcestershire's David Leatherdale will identify with the promise that in 1960

Portrait from 1960 © Coloursport.

an improvement in facilities for spectators was on the horizon. As today, the Supporters' Association was providing a boost to the overall finances of the club. In the fifty years since then financial issues still remain, as does the loyalty of the Supporters' Association.

The summer turned out to be a very wet one which hindered ambitions on and off the pitch, however, Worcestershire won two more games than in 1959 and rose one place to thirteenth. While there was no dramatic sign of what was to follow in the next few seasons, it appeared that the tide had turned. Five batsmen passed a thousand first class runs and while the fast improving Jack Flavell finished with 121 wickets, the spin department was beginning to take shape with Norman Gifford, Doug Slade and Martin Horton claiming nearly 200 wickets between them. Of this current crop of players, eight were to feature in the side which won the Championship four years later.

While two quick bowlers, Derek Pearson and John Aldridge, were to fade out of view after 1960, John recalls pre-season training with some amusement and how he managed to dodge getting involved:

> One day after practice we were told 'bring your running shoes tomorrow'; we are going to run up the Malverns. The British Camp pub was at the foot of the Malverns so when we arrived two senior pros told me to hold back, and while the others set off and we popped in for a couple of beers. When they got back the others asked us where the hell we had been. The two senior pros quickly said, 'We told you John that they had gone up the hill, and you said they went the other way.' We hadn't even run 10 yards in truth but just about got away with it.

John is still a regular visitor to New Road in the summer, now eighty years old he looks as fit as when he played, carries no weight and tells a good story or two over a pint in the Graeme Hick Pavilion. One thing with John is you can always say that he has a great day out whenever he watches cricket!

Don began the season in indifferent form with a run of low scores and, for the first six matches, batted in the unaccustomed position of either four of five in the order. A defeat against Glamorgan at Pontypridd in the opener was followed by the visit of South Africa to New Road. Roy McLean was the key performer for South Africa, he rattled up 207 before being dismissed by Len Coldwell. Seven second innings wickets from Atholl McKinnon dismissed the home-side for a poor 141 resulting in a 133 run defeat.

A first win came against Gloucestershire at Bristol with wickets for Flavell, Coldwell and Slade resulting in a 62 run margin of victory. The next visitors to New Road were Kent, which meant the return of, Peter Richardson to the County he captained a few years earlier; he had been out of cricket since 1958. Kent romped home by an innings and 92 runs mainly thanks to a first innings 125 not out by Alan Dixon batting at number seven. George Stokes, writing for the *Birmingham Mail*'s Sports Final, described the game:

> When Kent were hammering home their advantage in the game at New Road, Peter Richardson made no attempt to conceal his delight, yet he confessed to me that his pleasure was not as complete as it could have been. He was of the opinion

that it was asking too much of Kenyon to saddle him with two comparatively new players in Headley and Spencer and one completely new player in Standen.

It's also interesting to note the crowd's indifference towards Peter. The article continued, 'If Peter expected any kind of welcome on his return to the ground where he made his name he must have been bitterly disappointed. There was no cheering when he turned out with the rest of the Kent players to field in Worcestershire's first innings; nor when he opened Kent's reply with Arthur Phebey.' It would appear that a lukewarm reception for some former players is not a new phenomenon!

A four wicket win over Northamptonshire at Dudley was a welcome victory. Although Don only scored 33 in the first innings he was back to his familiar position of opener in the absence of Martin Horton. Described in the *Birmingham Mail* as 'Kenyon – brief, bright and breezy', his 33 was his highest score for nearly a month. Pleasingly though, he had been severe on Frank Tyson, hitting him for six and four boundaries to show a glimpse of a possible return to better times.

The financial position of the club was again in the spotlight when Don commented in the *Birmingham Mail* about the importance the Supporters' Association had in providing invaluable support: 'Worcestershire's Association is a leading example. Something like £80,000 has been spent on additional amenities in the last ten years. It has involved a lot of hard work on the part of a loyal band of volunteer workers who must be pleased with what they have accomplished as are the players and public for whom they have catered so lavishly.' The work of the Supporters' Association continues to go from strength to strength. In August 2014, two areas of new seating, paid for by the Association (the Brookes Supporters' Stand and the Mills Supporters' Stand) were unveiled in memory of Bob Brookes and Pat Mills, who served on the Association committee for many years.

Defeats against Gloucestershire and Lancashire followed in the last week of May, the second fixture serving as the benefit game for Worcestershire stalwart, George Dews. Set to retire the following season, George scored over 16,000 runs including twenty centuries and was one of the best close fielders to play for Worcestershire adding 353 catches to his career statistics.

At the start of June Don's much awaited first ton of the season arrived in the game against Essex at Romford and not before time. Putting on 207 for the first wicket, Ron Headley scored his maiden first class hundred (108) as Don reached exactly 100. It proved to be a tense finish as Essex held on for a draw when the visitors could only reach 64 – 5 off 11 overs in pursuit of a victory target of 66. During the match against Cambridge University at the end of June, Ron was given a bat, subscribed for by members of the club which was presented to him by Don and Cambridge University wicketkeeper/captain, Christopher Howland.

At this point, I recall part of my conversation I had with Ron during the winter of 2013. He said how happy he had been playing at Worcester, which is why he excelled:

Presentation bat to Ron Headley to celebrate his first first-class hundred. With Ron and Don is Christopher Howland, the Cambridge University wicketkeeper/captain. © Berrows Newspapers.

I fell in love with the ground as soon as I saw it. I should have gone to Warwickshire really because Dave Taylor, who played a lot with dad, was the coach there. I used to go to nets at Edgbaston and it was accepted I'd go there; however, I went to Worcester at the age of fourteen and loved it. I sat there day dreaming ... sat there towards the scoreboard under the trees and dreamt of being able to play a match out there. Years later it came to happen, it's a tranquil setting, a spiritual place. I had a bonding with the spectators because of how I went about my game.

I asked Ron about Don's ability to captain a side, he replied,

He had a lot of strong characters like Jack Flavell and Jim Standen and someone like Dick Richardson could be tricky to manage at times. His answer was to manage us like men. He said, 'You are all men and I'll treat you as such. I expect you to run your life in some sort of order to give your best on the pitch. What you do after I don't care if you want to go out boozing that's no problem but I want you with me next morning.'

Many of Don's contemporaries described him as a good, honest Black Country bloke, who said it as it was. This is a prime example of his straightforward, no nonsense approach to the game:

In later years Don would say 'Young Ron' – he always called me young Ron – 'you have the shots, go out and play, it's as simple as that.' When that comes from your captain it's a real bonus. He knew exactly what he was about. He wanted the best from you but appreciated only you could give of your best; he gave you the responsibility to produce your maximum level of performance. If he could get all eleven players doing that he knew we would steam roller them.

Don's resurgent form continued in the next game, a draw against Surrey with 110 in the first innings. It drew an unusual headline in *The People* on 12 June, it read: 'Century Maker Don Warns Middlesex'. It went on to say, 'Worcestershire batsman Don Kenyon needs one more to complete an all-round record. The hundred he got against Surrey in midweek means that he's now scored a century off every county but one; Middlesex. "Don't worry; their time will come" promises Don.' Sadly this record was never to fall. Despite scoring 12 fifties against Middlesex his top score was 90. Some years later the great Glenn Turner was to achieve this feat and like Don, he scored a hundred against 'his own' county a rare achievement to say the least. Just as Don was getting into his stride though, he missed the next three games with a badly bruised knee, therefore, George Dews took over the captaincy but a few days later probably wished he had not.

In a thrilling finish to the game at Old Trafford, Roy Booth finished 99 not out in the second innings to save the game, helping Worcestershire recover from 197 – 5 to 367 – 7. Overnight though the players had to make their way to the beautiful ground of Tunbridge Wells to play Kent. It was a red letter day too for Norman Gifford, he was about to make his first class debut with Worcestershire. The coach carrying the Worcestershire players arrived at the Spa Hotel in Tunbridge Wells at 4.00 a.m. in the middle of a torrential downpour and thunderstorm which was to have a big say on the outcome of the game.

Richard Walsh asked Colin Cowdrey to write the foreword to his 1993 book *All Over in a Day*, which described the outcome:

> A new groundsman, who proved to be a top notcher, was learning how best to master the square and he was not helped by the unsettled weather.
>
> Little did we realise what an extraordinary day lay ahead of us as groups of players stared at the mottled looking pitch, exchanging questioning glances. As the sun peeped through we could neither make head nor tail of it. The game took some unexpected turns and Kent ran out winners before the sun had gone down.

The scores were: Kent 187, Worcestershire 25 and following on, 61. The visitors had lost by an innings and 101 runs in less than a day, it was the last time that a first class game had started and finished on the same day.

Colin Cowdrey commented,

> George Dews shook my hand at the end with a wry smile and, fine cricketer and true sportsman that he was, showed a fine sense of humour saying, 'Let's play it all again tomorrow, on the same pitch, of course, but we must bat first.' With every

marquee fully booked, the caterers prepared, the ground looking glorious with the rhododendrons in full bloom, I rather think we should have done!

Don recovered from his knee injury during which time one game was won and one game lost. The win against Cambridge University was celebrated by Norman Gifford, who in only his second game, returned match figures of 10 – 59. Next up were Glamorgan at Stourbridge which once again saw the captain back to his very best and reunited with his opening partner, Martin Horton. Restricting the visitors to 255 (thanks to 5 – 37 from Jack Flavell) Worcestershire replied with 355 – 6 declared with Don's contribution being 201.

'Kenyon Hits out for Double Century' was the headline in the *Birmingham Post* on 1 July which commented,

> Anything more strangely contrasting than the displays of rival opening batsmen at Stourbridge yesterday could hardly be imagined. Kenyon showed all the artistry and all the skill of a master of his craft in scoring 201 out of Worcestershire's total of 356. Peter Walker, a stopgap opener for Glamorgan also had a fantastic hour of living dangerously while scoring 68 out of 81.

Peter Walker recalled this game in his 2006 book, *It's Not Just Cricket*, and is quoted:

> Returning from the euphoria at Lord's to Stourbridge, I made a miserable 5 in the first innings. Because of injury Wilf Wooller missed the game and our opening batsman Gilbert Parkhouse captained us. When he in turn injured his hand, he pushed me up the order to open in the second innings with Bernard Hedges. There was nothing pre-meditated about what happened next, but something inside me snapped.
>
> Worcestershire had a formidable attack: Jack Flavell, Fred Rumsey and John Aldridge, the first two going on to play for England. I stood firm footed at the crease and just slashed, heaved and slogged at every ball bowled at me. Somehow I connected more times than I missed and, to the accompaniment of oaths such as 'and you call yourself a fucking England player' from Don Kenyon, the ball flew everywhere, once even out of the ground! John Billot from the *Western Mail* called it one of the most startling displays ever of unorthodox batting by a Glamorgan player. I hit a six over Flavell's head and eleven fours and I was eventually caught by Kenyon off Rumsey for 68, scored inside an hour, out of a total of 81. So disgusted with my performance was my fastidious opening partner Bernard Hedges that he refused to talk to me out in the middle for some weeks thereafter.
>
> Many years later, at a dinner for former England players at the Café Royal in London, I sat next to Jack Flavell, one of the meanest, most hostile quick bowlers I ever played against. He somehow managed a tight smile and shook his head sadly as we relived that extraordinary innings. He left me in no doubt that even thirty years on it still rankled within his breast.

Jeff Jones who was also in the Glamorgan side had vivid memories of what happened:

I'd just gone in the side and remember that Ossie Wheatley had joined us from Warwickshire and was called up for the Gents versus Players game at Lords, so I came in at Stourbridge. Gilbert Parkhouse was captain and we put them into bat. Brian Evans, a ginger haired boy was opening the bowling and Don was facing. He hooked a bouncer to me at fine leg ... it went straight in ... and out ... he went on to make a double hundred. This was one of my first games as I'd only just made my debut at Blackheath against Kent. Gilbert Parkhouse said at end of play to try and bowl him out and we said that's what we'd been trying to do all day!

I used to watch Don play a lot, Ossie told me to watch from third man and see where the good players play, how they stand or hold the bat. Typically a top of the bat grip indicates a front foot player and a low grip signifies a back foot player. Don was a very good back foot player so I tried to keep him on the front foot.

I remember a few years later at Colwyn Bay, I'd just been selected for England and Don by then was one of the selectors, it was August time. Bas [Basil D'Oliveira] was in the Worcester side that day and both of us were selected for West Indies that winter. I opened the bowling and had him caught behind in the first over. I thanked him for selecting me and as he walked off he just smiled with a wry grin.

Worcestershire's form was inconsistent during the next nine games, recording four wins, three defeats and two losses. During that time, however, there were some outstanding individual performances:

> Martin Horton: 101 v Essex, 150 v Warwickshire and 159 v Sussex. Add to that his 6 – 94 in the Sussex game.
> Jack Flavell: 6 – 50 v Northants, 5 – 35 v Sussex and 6 – 93 v Warwickshire.
> George Dews: 124 against Essex
> Ron Hedley: Cracked his second century of the season with 107 versus Nottinghamshire.
> Len Coldwell: 5 – 109 against Essex.
> Norman Gifford: Showing signs of becoming a top class spinner, returned figures of 6 – 32 against Nottinghamshire.
> Doug Slade: First five wicket haul of the season with 6 – 23 against Nottinghamshire.

Signs of progress were evident as the team entered the last month of the season and Don was still not 'done' with his run scoring. He signed off with two more hundreds, the first being a typically hard hit 125 against Somerset at Kidderminster. 'Kenyon Hits 125 in Worcester Spree' was the headline in the *Sports Argus* which went on to report that if the game had not been interrupted by rain for fifteen minutes, Don would have completed his hundred before lunch. At the interval he was still only six runs short.

Another seven wicket haul from Martin Horton put Worcestershire in command, however, on the last day 115 not out from opener Graham Atkinson and 85 not out from Abbas Baig helped Somerset to a nine wicket victory. A second century in a week followed at Eastbourne, this time his 109 in the second innings helped Worcestershire to a 90 run victory. The *Daily Telegraph* ran the headline: 'Kenyon Dazzles with Another Great Century'. The report by their 'special correspondent' stated, 'Kenyon started with three boundaries off Bates' first over, and that was the standard he maintained for the whole of the 115 minutes up to close of play. It was a display fit to compare with that at Kidderminster last Saturday.'

While progress up the Championship table was slight, high quality individual performances were becoming more common place. Six batsmen passed the 1,000 run mark and while Jack Flavell was again the only bowler to claim 100 wickets, Doug Slade (92), Martin Horton (56) and Norman Gifford (31) were tilting the balance in favour of the slower bowler. This was an interesting development as many counties were heading down the 'pace attack' route but 1961 would be a challenge for all concerned.

Chapter 13

Onwards and Upwards

Following an encouraging second half to the previous season, 1961 was greeted with great optimism. Tom Graveney, one of the foremost batsmen of his generation, had signed from Gloucestershire, unfortunately, after the initial euphoria, in echoes of the Richardson affair a few years earlier, the MCC decided that he was not allowed to play championship matches until the following season. Consequently the great batsman spent much of the summer playing for Dudley in the Birmingham League.

Don was fast gaining a reputation as one of the best skippers and had at his disposal an attack of great impact and variety, probably the best in the country. More positive news came with Flavell's selection for the last two Tests against Australia. A disappointing downside was that after the two opening games Doug Slade broke an ankle playing football and missed the remainder of the season.

The Second XI, under the captaincy of Secretary Joe Lister, himself no mean cricketer, fared better than they had for many years by finishing fourth. Unfortunately, as part of the economic cutbacks the playing staff was reduced to eighteen and the services of Coach Charlie Hallows, the former Lancashire batsman, were dispensed with during the season. He was later to re-join the County.

In early April the *Evening News and Times* ran a revealing feature about the season ahead when Don called for an 'all-out effort from the players'. It went on to state, 'When Worcestershire county cricketers reported for their first pre-season practice today, their captain, Don Kenyon told them they were expected by the committee to make a 100 per cent effort to play bright and attractive cricket in a bid to win back the crowds.'

Don echoed this:

Cricket is at a crossroads and no opportunity must be lost to speed up the game wherever possible in accordance with the instructions we have received from the MCC. W. R. Chignell is quoted: 'The Hon Dick Lygon as chair of the cricket sub-committee was responsible, with Kenyon and Hallows, for increasing the discipline of the side with the result that Worcestershire were a happy team, as will always be the case when firm but not oppressive discipline is exercised'.

If the opening game against Australia was anything to go by then the season would be a tremendous one. It proved to be the Club's best and closest attempt to beat the visitors since they first played them in 1902 as Martin Horton with 5 – 46 helped bowl out Australia for 177. The last eight wickets had fallen for 86 and this proved to be their lowest total ever against Worcestershire. In reply Worcestershire were rushed out for just 155 with Ken Mackay claiming 4 – 14. Jack Flavell soon removed both visiting openers and then an inspired spell of 5 – 45 from Len Coldwell reduced the Aussies to 141 all out. Only Neil Harvey with 37 drew any credit from the innings but he fell to a poor shot and was bowled by Gifford.

Chasing 163 to win, both the Worcestershire innings and the outcome of the match were delicately poised at 56 – 4 when rain came, meaning an early abandonment to the game. Still, Worcestershire had shown the positive intent called for just a few weeks earlier and had achieved it in front of a 12,000 crowd on day one.

In October 2014 I wrote to Richie Benaud and enclosed a copy of the picture of him and Don as a reminder of the game. I asked him for his observations about Don, his batting and his captaincy, below is his response. Probably not feeling his best, it's the mark of the man that he took time to reply, here is his e-mail in its entirety:

> Thank you for your letter and the memories of the opening matches of the 1953, 1956 and 1961 tours. I'm sorry I'm unable to be of any great assistance with replies to your questions.
>
> In 1953 we arrived in bleak conditions in the team bus from East Molesey and Don created his own record by hitting the first century against any Australian team. I was lucky enough to share a century partnership with Keith Miller who himself made a double century; great fun for a youngster.
>
> More fun in the 1956 match where I made runs and there was a wonderful end to the match when Jack Flavell played out the last three balls of the match for a draw. No fun at all in 1961 because I had badly damaged ligaments in my bowling shoulder.
>
> I hope all goes well for you and I remember Don as one of the great gentlemen of the game, as well as a fine player.
>
> Kind regards, Richie

In the opening exchanges in the Championship, the County made an encouraging start. Three wins, two draws and just the one defeat against Kent at home was more than acceptable. In the return game against Kent at Gravesend during the last week of May, Don scored his first ton of the season being dismissed by David Halfyard for 114. In a close finish time got the better of the visitors who closed on 184 – 6 needing just 38 more to win.

In the *Birmingham Mail* Don wrote of his frustration at not quite getting to the target but shared his sympathy for his good friend Martin Horton who was playing for the MCC against The Australians at Lord's. He said, 'Martin had the misfortune to bag a pair which was, in fact, a queen pair. For the uninitiated it means he was out first ball first innings and second ball second innings!' True to form, Martin bounced back with 108 in the following Championship game against Sussex.

During this time, the attacking cricket which was promised yielded two victories and three defeats. The bowlers continued to take their wickets and

Don with Australian Captain Richie Benaud in 1961 © Mirrorpix.

Worcestershire vs Australia, 1961. © Coloursport.

there were more runs for Horton, Headley and Tom Graveney who struck an elegant 152 not out in one of his rare appearances in the 112 run win against Cambridge University.

Don's second hundred came in the 233 run victory over Somerset at Don's favourite ground, Dudley; a place where inevitably he scored heavily. Mike Langley's headline in *The People* read: 'Kenyon Hits 152'. He went on to explain,

> Somerset skipper Harold Stephenson owned the reddest face in county cricket last night. He put Worcestershire in at Dudley – and they hit 394 runs – for five wickets declared.
>
> Worcester skipper Don Kenyon, as soon as he had recovered from the surprise, smashed twenty-one boundaries and 152 runs in 230 minutes. And young Ron Headley, Kenyon's partner in a 170 run second wicket stand that defied six bowlers, pounded 150 too.

When the partnership was broken, they had put on 220 for the second wicket. In reply, 5 – 72 from Len Coldwell restricted Somerset to 236 and following a declaration at 199 – 4, Worcestershire set the visitors 357 to win. Jack Flavell with 6 – 46 from 15 overs routed the visitors for just 124 to secure a win by 233 runs.

Ron Headley said,

> Don was good at spotting the ability of players and maximising it using a common sense approach. At the time I could murder anything on the on the leg side but had problems on the offside. During practice I got them to bowl on the offside and refused to play on the leg side, this was because my eye facing the ball was lazy and so I worked out how to do it.

I continued by asking Ron what made Don so respected as a person, to which he needed no time to think. As he started talking again his face lit up once more, he obviously held him in very high regard:

> The advice he gave me in 1958 was invaluable when I went to see Joe Lister with my uncle, Sid Stone. He owned the Swan pub in Dudley and I lived with him and regard him as one of my four earthly fathers. I signed and Joe Lister looked across the desk, 'young man I wish you all the best, do you have a bank account? I want to be able to pay you!'
>
> I said I wasn't starting until April, but he wanted to pay me all year round because there was no signing on fee and they didn't want me to go to Warwickshire. He paid me £48 per month which I thought was strange because I wasn't playing cricket. Joe and my uncle must have agreed it.
>
> Don then said, 'Ron, don't be like the rest of them, they go on the dole in the winter. My advice is to do something that you like doing as a job of work and get accomplished at it.' I went into the car industry, it was one of the best bits of advice I ever had. Once more this was fatherly advice from Don.

The next three games were drawn followed by a defeat at the hands of Somerset at Knowle in Bristol, but then the County embarked on a hot streak of seven consecutive victories. During that time, Don only mustered 260 runs and did not score another century for the remainder of the season. In spite of this, the side played some outstanding, attacking cricket and as an outside bet, were possible contenders for the Championship for the very first time in its history. These were heady days.

There were some exceptional performances during this time, they have been summarised below:

Headley 103 vs Derbyshire
Coldwell 8 – 41 vs Derbyshire
Coldwell 5 – 18 vs Glamorgan
Broadbent 102 vs Northamptonshire
Horton 7 – 42 vs Northamptonshire
Horton 6 – 60 vs Middlesex
Flavell 8 – 43 vs Lancashire

Sadly the bubble burst in the game against Yorkshire at Bradford starting on 16 August. Don missed this game with tonsillitis and the side was further depleted with injury to Vice-Captain George Dews and Jack Flavell away playing with England. To make matters worse Fred Trueman had been omitted from the England team so was determined to make his point.

In the absence of Kenyon and Dews, Roy Booth captained the side. With scores of just 124 and 169 his team was no match for Yorkshire's 306 all out and the County subsided to defeat by an innings and 13 runs. Trueman was the destroyer in the second innings with 5 – 46 from 24 overs. Norman Gifford recalled vividly another game against Yorkshire in 1964 when Fred was at his most fiery:

I remember Don getting hold of Trueman and smacking him all around New Road; then this beamer came. Don was a sportsman but this day he walked up to Fred, showed him his bat and in effect said to him 'now you bugger off back to your mark, bowl me another like that and I'll wrap this round your head.' If Don did that he meant it; he was a hard bugger. He played the game properly, but when the line was over stepped that was a different matter. I've never seen anyone play the quicks better!

Even now, if you say such and such is a good player of spin they are, but it's comfortable. If you ask anyone do you like it flying around your ear-holes? Do they like it? Buggery. How can anyone fancy that happening, but Don was in his element when it did.

It was suggested that Don had even 'invited' Fred to meet him at the back of the pavilion after close of play for a punch up, he was that incensed by the incident. Tom Graveney remarked,

Nobody would try it on with Don, you wouldn't take liberties with him; he was well respected to a man. He liked taking it out on Yorkshire probably because he disliked them; it was a fixture where he always seemed to raise his game.

He was in charge and the players knew that. Don never asked people what to
do, they just did it. He too was highly responsible for everything he did and he
would never cheat; the players respected that.

The run in to the climax of the 1961 season continued and to the players' credit,
they bounced back with an eight wicket victory against Nottinghamshire at
Trent Bridge. Yet again, Len Coldwell took wickets and turned in figures of 5
– 101 in the first innings, while George Dews' 113 gave the visitors a one run
advantage on first innings. In one of only six appearances for Worcestershire,
Staffordshire born Alan Duff, claimed 4 – 51 in the Nottinghamshire second
innings to leave Worcestershire 195 to win. The ever dependable Martin Horton
finished on 106 not out and in a quick fire partnership with Bob Broadbent (54
not out) put on 151 unbroken for the third wicket.

Don was back for the draw with Middlesex and for the win of the season
over Surrey at The Oval. In response to Surrey's 266, the visitors were bundled
out for 90 thanks to 6 – 25 from Richard Jefferson. With a rule change in 1961
not permitting the follow on, Surrey batted again and declared on 196 – 6 to set
Worcestershire an unlikely victory target of 372.

Progressing towards the target there were useful contributions from Horton
(40) Headley (45) and Norman Gifford, batting at number five who scored
35. The star of the show, however, was Dick Richardson who scored his first
hundred for two seasons, a majestic 165 not out to steer Worcestershire home
by three wickets.

Richardson's performance was typical of his ability and was aptly described
by Mike Vockins in his *Worcestershire CCC Pictorial History* when he said,
'Dick Richardson as a cricketer was something of an enigma, but what an
attractive and delightful enigma. When the side was in trouble his combative
and indomitable spirit showed.' Never were these words truer than after this
innings. For the defeat against Lancashire Don dropped himself down the order
to number six to allow Dick Richardson the chance to open, disappointingly
though, Don's own form was not at its best. Batting at five in the final game, a
victory over Sussex at Hove, he only recorded scores of 2 and 0. The hero this
time was Norman Gifford with match figures of 10 – 65.

Dropping himself down the order was an unusual move for Don,
something which Alan Ormrod picked up on when I spoke with him: 'Don
was a consistent man in everything he did. I only ever saw him have self-
doubts about his batting once and that was in the final match of 1961 when he
went down to five in the order. It didn't work, it's the only time I remember
him struggling but it didn't last long and in 1962 he opened again. Sometimes
the more you work the worse you get.'

A revealing article in the *Sports Argus* on the opening day of the Sussex game
hinted that Don might consider a permanent move to a lower position in the
batting order, he was quoted: 'I've got to consider the team's interests. I shall not
make a definite decision until nearer next season but I have been considering it
seriously for some time. It's been a wonderful season and we have played some
wonderful cricket.' Norman Whiting told me that Don confided in him that if
he had not always put the interests of the team first he could well have scored

a hundred first class hundreds. That we shall never know, but it underlines his ethos of putting the team first

As a footnote the Supporters' Association came in for special praise too. They found the money needed to retain Charlie Hallows as coach for the next season following his temporary departure earlier in the year for financial reasons.

Don finished the campaign with 1,399 runs at 25.43 with just the two hundreds, while the team finished a creditable fourth position. As the season closed, four bowlers – Jack Flavell, Len Coldwell, Martin Horton and Norman Gifford – all took 100 first class wickets, the first time this had been achieved since Reg Perks, Syd Martin, Dick Howorth and Peter Jackson achieved it in 1937.

Martin Horton: 101 wickets at 21. 64
Len Coldwell: 140 wickets at 19.25
Norman Gifford: 133 wickets at 19.66
Jack Flavell: 171 wickets at 17.79

The other outstanding achievement belonged to 'young Ron' – Ron Headley – who in a magnificent season became the youngest Worcestershire batsman to score 2,000 runs in a season. This was a record held until Graeme Hick beat it in 1986.

Chapter 14

Nearly but not Quite and a Vintage Century

As early as January 1962 Tony Cox, writing his 'sports gossip' column for the *Express and Star,* delivered the headline: 'An SOS from CCC – Target 2,000 at Worcester'. Deciphering the code, the harsh reality was that the club was in a perilous financial state once more.

Jack Sellars, chairman of the new membership committee revealed, 'Our income has dropped and our expenditure has risen. This is a disturbing trend which must be tackled at once.' In his straightforward and blunt message Don stated, 'If our supporters do not rally round, in a few years the Worcestershire Club will be dead. The target of the club is another 2,000 members who would each plough in three guineas to the club coffers.' President and local industrialist, Sir George Dowty commented, 'We have never really tackled our membership problem before, but it's obvious that county clubs must help themselves if they are to survive.' The message was loud and clear, if things were to improve off the pitch then the entertainment on it had to be first class. Apart from George Dews, who had retired, the same players were available as, crucially, was Tom Graveney, who had spent the previous season qualifying.

Jack Flavell began the season in magnificent form and had claimed 89 wickets by the second week of July. He then strained an achilles tendon and missed the rest of the season. In addition, Ron Headley broke a wrist while Horton, Coldwell and Broadbent all missed matches through illness or injury. It proved to be the most memorable season on record, with the champions not being crowned until the last day of the season. That said, Worcestershire should have had the title in the bag well before then. On 15 August they failed by 8 runs, with only one wicket left, to beat Derbyshire at Chesterfield when set 111 to win in 124 minutes. This was followed by two frustrating drawn games against Leicestershire which only yielded four points. It was these results which cost them the title.

The highlight of the drawn game with the Pakistan tourists was the second innings 117 from Tom Graveney, who was last man dismissed when run out. The other encouraging element was that the three seamers, Flavell, Coldwell and Jim Standen were all among the wickets. Standen was to claim five wickets (5 – 48) in the next Championship game, a draw against Sussex at Hove.

I spoke to Jim Standen in 2005 just after his 70th birthday. After many years of searching I had tracked him down to his home in America. He told me:

Do you know I'm exactly the same weight today as when I played cricket, it's amazing. I have a good lifestyle really; I live in a great place called Walnut Creek in California and play a round of golf every day of the week. My wife has a good job in banking, so from time to time we have to move, that's why it's sometimes hard to reach me still, and I have no complaints doing what I do every day.

Another drawn game against Glamorgan afforded Duncan Fearnley a first-class debut while Don scored his second half-century of the campaign. An entry in the Club's 1963 Yearbook describing how the 'boundaries flowed from his bat'. A slight injury to Don meant that Duncan had the chance to open in the second innings and he struck a stylish 30 with some well-timed and attractive shots.

Duncan has been a stalwart of Worcestershire cricket for over fifty years. A former chairman and president, he was instrumental in changing the attitude and ambition of the club when he signed Ian Botham and Graham Dilley in 1987. His other skill, of course, is as a craftsman, rare in the ability to 'hand splice' a cricket bat. Used and known all around the world, his bats are still recognised to this day. In conversation with him during the 2014 season, Duncan described Don as a fearless cricketer and captain and if he said jump, you jumped. One particular tale he recalled was after the end of the 1961 season:

We had Fred Rumsey on the books at one time, a left arm quick and a big fella. Don let him go at the end of '61 and he went to Somerset after a couple of years. Fred disliked Don profusely for sacking him and never forgot it.

　　We played against Somerset at Worcester, he'd not long got in the England team to play in England, but he wasn't then picked to tour Australia. Don apparently didn't think he had the fitness to stand up to it and he told Alec Bedser, his co-selector and chairman at the time. Fred heard about this and on a red hot day at New Road we played Somerset where I was due in at six and Don was down to open with Martin (Horton). The day finished at 7.00 p.m. then and we had fielded nearly all day and I'd been running around for most of it, when Somerset's innings closed. I thought I'd get to the back of the queue as we left the field and walked straight through the dressing room and into the toilet in the corridor. I locked the door and waited for the bell to go, by which time Don and Martin would be ready to go out. I waited but all of a sudden there's a knock on the toilet door and a voice said, 'Duncan this is your captain speaking. You can take the honours tonight, I'm absolutely knackered.' I said 'I am too Captain, and you're a better player than me.' Anyhow, I had to rush and get my pads on and dashed out with Martin. Martin took first ball and Fred came charging in from Diglis End. To make it worse there was no sightscreen then, Martin fended one off to fine leg so I was on strike and as a left-armer Fred was bowling over the wicket. He hit me straight on the temple, it went over Bill Alley's head at gully and I got four leg byes. We didn't survive too long the next morning.

Duncan is a great storyteller, time in his company is always good fun and an education. The encouraging start to the 1962 season turned into an excellent one over the next two months during which time eight games (including a win over Oxford University) were won and five were drawn. Tom Graveney steered

Worcestershire to an impressive six wicket victory over Middlesex at Lord's with a classy 119 (his first in the Championship for his new county) which was well supported with 63 not out from Dick Richardson.

The headline in the *Express and Star* read: 'Kenyon and Horton make Merry'. A quick fire start from both openers had given Graveney, Richardson and Headley the chance to attack the bowling which they did with great zest. In the *Birmingham Mail* Don paid tribute to Tom by stating, 'The most pleasing aspect of the win at headquarters was the magnificent form of Tom Graveney. It was Graveney at his best and everyone knows how good that can be. When he gets going Tom always impresses me as the finest stroke player in the country.'

A win at Northamptonshire by 118 runs followed, Martin Horton (105) and Len Coldwell (6 – 63) taking the spoils. It became three on the bounce with a nine wicket thumping of Kent at New Road and despite a second innings 113 from Colin Cowdrey, the seamers did the damage and shared the wickets once more. The next game, however, was the big test, Yorkshire the leaders were the visitors to Worcester.

Still awaiting his first century of the season, Don was accounted for by Fred Trueman and in front of large crowds the game was drawn. Worcestershire had fought hard, with Alex Bannister describing the Yorkshire effort in the *Daily Mail*: 'Set to make 229 in 2 hours 53 minutes, Yorkshire soon showed the extent of their ambition was a draw. Yorkshire stumbled to 103 – 7 with the eighth wicket pair of Trueman and Don Wilson ringed by fielders, edging nervously through the extra period.' It had denied Worcestershire ten valuable points, all which served to send Surrey back to the top of the table.

The attacking style of cricket was never more in evidence than at Trent Bridge. 'Kenyon sparkles in last hour' was the report in the *Birmingham Post* while 'Kenyon shames Notts bats' was the headline in the *Daily Mail*. It read, 'Nottinghamshire took five and a quarter hours to crawl to 209, but in 65 minutes to the close, Worcestershire raced to 71 without loss. Skipper Don Kenyon completed his 50 (8 fours and a six) in the last over.' The form was there but the big score was not. When the season closed Don had scored two centuries and fourteen half-centuries, a disappointing conversion rate for a player of his ability.

In Nottinghamshire's second innings, Jim Standen tore through the batting with 6 – 32 from just 16 overs, which meant the visitors had the easy task of knocking off the 65 runs to claim a nine wicket victory. Unfortunately for Don he was out for a duck caught by Bill Rhodes – father of Steve Rhodes, the former Worcestershire wicketkeeper and now their Director of Cricket, off John Cotton.

The batting continued to flourish with back to back hundreds for Dick Richardson with both Tom Graveney and Bob Broadbent chipping in with a ton each. At Romford against Essex an innings and 172 run victory was achieved thanks to Jack Flavell with figures of 6 – 45 and 5 – 38. Len Coldwell bagged the other 9 to round off a brilliant display of new ball bowling. The record books were out during the game against Somerset at New Road as a result of some phenomenal batting. Having first use of one of groundsman Mike Biddle's pitches, which could be known to be a bit spicy, in two and a half hours the home-side scored 172 – 2 of which Don had pasted Somerset for 97 in 107 minutes. Ken Palmer bowled him 8 minutes before the lunch interval when a ton in the first session beckoned. One milestone was reached, as during the innings he passed 30,000 first class runs.

Ironically at the toss, both captains came to the conclusion that the pitch was unfit for play. In Andy Murtagh's *Touched by Greatness, The Story of Tom Graveney*, Tom commented, 'The pitch did look awful. Hasty telephone calls were made to Lord's in an effort to get the game postponed but the powers that be at headquarters were adamant in their ruling; the game must proceed as scheduled at all costs.' It was widely acknowledged that Don was a great reader of pitches, something I discussed with Mike Vockins. Mike recalls one incident from 1965, 'We were due to play Hampshire so Don went to the ground the night before, saw the pitch and told Mick Biddle it was too good. As a result, he got some of the boys to walk up and down with their spikes on. I questioned this some years later when I was talking to Ted Hemsley about it. Ted said it was correct, he was one of the boys.'

The fun against Somerset in 1962 didn't stop there. W. R. Chignell described the action,

> Kenyon's example set Horton and Graveney on fire and these two put on 314 together which was a record for the County. Kenyon hit 16 fours in his scintillating innings and Horton, whose 233 was the highest score in English cricket in 1962 and also his personal best, hit no less than 36 fours. Graveney went on a little longer and was 164 not out, with a six and 21 fours when Kenyon declared at 520 – 3.

With Secretary Joe Lister and Groundsman Mike Biddle. © Mirrorpix.

The *Express and Star* described the day as 'positively bristling with handsome stroke making and so savage was the Worcestershire assault that they were still able to get Somerset in for 70 minutes batting before the close.' Five wickets in the first innings from Len Coldwell (5 – 47) and four from Norman Gifford in the second innings (4 – 29) resulted in Worcestershire cruising to a win by 264 runs.

Worcestershire's third wicket partnership record stood until 1997. I was in Southampton at the time, so when Worcestershire were in town I needed no excuse to go to Northlands Road to watch the game. I recall Graeme Hick (303 not out) and Tom Moody (180 not out) demolishing a hugely inexperienced Hampshire opening attack to put on 434 unbroken for the third wicket. Both Tom and Martin were at the game to see the record books re-written. The bats used in this innings by Tom and Graeme are now on display in the pavilion at New Road. Needing a tidy sum of money to buy them, the Worcestershire CCC Heritage Group put out an appeal to raise funds in order to buy these unique items of memorabilia and in less than 48 hours the deal was done thanks to the generosity of the Worcestershire supporters.

Don's first hundred of 1962 eventually arrived in the pulsating game at Old Trafford, a game which went down to the wire. A first innings 102 not out from Roy Booth gave Worcestershire a first innings lead of 106 but with Geoff 'Noddy' Pullar scoring 155 in Lancashire's second knock, the visitors were left to get 196 in just over 2 hours. The desire to attack and win games rather than hold out for a draw was never more evident. The first 50 came in 34 minutes and the 100 was up in 67 minutes, but after Martin Horton was dismissed the remaining batsmen could not match the tempo. Despite this, Don continued to rattle along and was 106 not out at the close with Worcestershire an agonising 15 runs short. Kenyon's vintage innings had contained 8 fours, and 4 sixes in his stay at the crease of 108 minutes.

It took just two days to brush aside Glamorgan at Neath with Flavell (5 – 27) and Standen (5 – 26) destroying the home-side. The pleasing thing for the skipper writing in the *Birmingham Mail* was that 'it was the more remarkable for the fact that the victory was achieved on a very good wicket which gave little help to the bowlers.'

Standen's form during the summer was to earn him his county cap while the promising Alan Ormrod received his Second XI cap. A strong second team invariably means a strong first team, ultimately the seconds, under the captaincy of Joe Lister went on to win the title. Sadly, the bubble burst in the next game where Northamptonshire were the visitors to Kidderminster. It proved to be the County's first defeat of the season which had reached early July. Another Tom Graveney hundred (110) was not enough to hold back Brian Crump (6 – 86 and 4 – 44) plus Michael Norman who scored 116 and 76.

Normal service was resumed at Stourbridge where a second innings 111 not out from Martin Horton saw Worcestershire home by nine wickets inside two days against Lancashire. Unfortunately, the tables were turned when Warwickshire visited New Road and inflicted a two day defeat on the home-side.

Watched by the biggest crowds of the season, the two sides were neck and neck at the top of the table. Dismissed for 99 – having been 88 for 3 and 184, thanks to a technically sound innings of 76 from Don the runs were insufficient to prevent Warwickshire winning by five wickets. Candid as ever, Don's column in the *Birmingham Mail* said it all when he was quoted, 'We only had ourselves to blame and to put it mildly I'm disappointed.'

Norman Gifford turned in match figures of 11 – 71 in the victory over Somerset at Bath followed by a draw with Warwickshire in a very low scoring game at Edgbaston with Bob Carter turning in the star performance with 5 – 55 in Warwickshire's first innings.

The 30 run defeat at Gloucester appeared to be a pivotal moment in the season, with some pinpointing this game as the reason why Worcestershire did not go on to win the Championship. Graveney and Gifford were away playing a representative game at Lord's and Flavell and Headley were injured, so four capped players were absent.

The problem was not with the reserves, but rather the more established players who did not fire. The exception was Roy Booth who was left stranded on 99 not out in the first innings, with the other highlight being 58 from Alan Ormrod in only his second Championship outing. Stand in Fred Rumsey was the pick of the bowlers with 5 – 37 but these efforts were not enough to prevent the inevitable.

With Sussex the visitors to New Road at the end of July, Don was out to impress Sussex captain 'Lord' Ted Dexter, who had also been appointed as MCC captain for the upcoming winter tour of Australia. With Horton, Gifford and Slade sharing eight wickets, Sussex were dismissed for 197. In reply, half-centuries from Broadbent (83) and Ormrod (59), Worcestershire took a lead of 113 on first innings. 5 – 35 from Martin Horton meant that the team needed just 50 to win, they got there without loss.

Ian Wooldridge writing for the *Daily Mail* wrote the telling headline: 'The Sauce of it – Limping Worcester Top'. He went on, 'Mighty Ted Dexter, trapped like a caged tiger by the finest spin bowling I have seen this season was powerless last night, as maimed, mauled Worcestershire clawed their way back to the top of the County Championship.' He paid tribute to the side missing the four capped players and Roy Booth who had to retire hurt with an eye injury. Wooldridge intimated that; 'The match turned on Norman Gifford who walked off with nothing more remarkable than 1 – 47. In the second innings he had tied Dexter down for over half an hour, only for him to lose patience and be bowled by Bob Carter for 3.

A draw at The Oval against Surrey was followed by another victory, this time by five wickets over Derbyshire at Dudley. Len Coldwell with 8 – 64 from 20 overs was the destroyer and restricted the visitors to 97. Worcestershire, however, only limped to 149 but with Standen, Carter and Gifford sharing the wickets second time around, Worcestershire required 187 to win and got there with Don scoring 89.

Rain ruined the outcome of the well poised 'return fixture' against Surrey, *The Evening News and Times* recounting the early exchanges with the headline: 'Worcestershire Top Dogs – County Pacemen Send Surrey Reeling'. 4 – 44 from Len Coldwell and 5 – 48 from Bob Carter (including Peter May for a polished 55) bowled Surrey out for 146. Carrying forward a 20 run lead on first innings, Doug Slade chipped in with 6 – 43 and Surrey were dismissed for 170 second time around.

The *Express and Star's* headline read: 'Worcester want 148 to Win' but, the weather had the last shout and the game was drawn without the fourth innings getting underway. Sadly, the weather intervened again in the Bank Holiday game with Essex, although with a deficit of 84 in a low scoring first innings, it might have been a blessing in disguise that the second innings did not commence!

The run in to the end of the season had begun and even *The Times* was hinting at 'Worcestershire's chance of first title' ... but could it be done? In the home game against Hampshire, Alex Bannister's headline in the *Daily Mail* summed up the mounting tension: 'Kenyon banks on brainpower.' In the article he stated that 'Kenyon, who cannot afford a tactical mistake as the season reaches its climax, gambled on his knowledge of the Worcester pitch – and won. He put Hampshire in to bat to give them the worst of a saturated pitch.'

With all of the bowlers sharing the wickets, it was Tom Graveney who gave one of his most majestic displays and won an intriguing battle with the country's leading wicket-taker Derek Shackleton. Graveney's 106 was his ninth century of the season, highlighting his worth to the team. More success for the bowling attack resulted in Worcestershire getting home by nine wickets; it also took them back to the top of the table.

The weather had the final say in the top of the table clash with Yorkshire at Headingley with Dick Richardson scoring 102, but when the weather closed in, Worcestershire were 107 behind on first innings and facing an uphill battle. At least any damage to their title push had been kept to a minimum.

 Although an eleven wicket haul for Fred Rumsey (4 – 46 and 7 – 50) was not enough to force a win against Derbyshire at Chesterfield, it was a game which Worcestershire should have won. The *Saturday Sports News* summed it up well by reporting that 'County batsmen slip up badly at Chesterfield'. Requiring just 110 for victory, they stumbled to 103 – 9 with Gifford and Carter surviving the last 7 minutes of the game with a victory tantalisingly close. This result alone was to have the greatest impact on the outcome of the championship.

A second consecutive draw, this time against Leicestershire once more tilted the balance of the title. Don (74) and Martin Horton (92) went off like rockets to put on 160 for the first wicket and were well supported by Dick Richardson with 95 to back up his 89 at Chesterfield, to signal a welcome return to form just at the right time of the season. Worcestershire could not break down the home team's resistance in the second innings and even a few overs of donkey drops and occasional spin from Graveney and Ormrod could not force the issue.

The following day, the return fixture began at Leicestershire. Six consecutive days play against the same opponents and two declarations (at last!) still could not produce a result in a game affected by rain. Meanwhile, Yorkshire produced another win to go back to the top of the table in what was proving to be a most exciting climax to the season. In a precursor to the penultimate game, Don wrote honestly in his regular column for the *Birmingham Mail*. The headline: 'What a Time to Slip' said it all. He commented, 'Our strong batting has faltered.' Only two individual hundreds had been scored since the first defeat of the season at the start of July and the previously 'hot' batting witnessed in the first two months of the season had cooled somewhat. Don was also still searching for his very best form; one hundred for the season to date was not his best return.

His perception of the situation was evident when he went on to state, 'At such a critical phase of the Championship fight no department can afford to be off form. That has been the secret of Yorkshire's success; someone always comes good at the right moment.' A solid batting card rather than a spectacular one was sufficient to get home against Gloucestershire by 134 runs. Don with 58, Horton with 95, and a 50 in each innings from Richardson gave Worcestershire the edge. Len Coldwell blew the opposition away twice with figures of 7 – 33 and 5 – 63.

Going into the last game there was still a chance that the title could be secured but a strong performance was needed. The equation was simple, if Worcestershire beat Nottinghamshire, Yorkshire would have to win their last game against Glamorgan. Having had the visitors 96 – 7 Nottinghamshire recovered to 193 all out thanks to 61 from Alan Gill and 51 from keeper Geoff Millman. At 118 – 6 Worcestershire were in trouble but the fighting spirit did not desert them in their hour of need. 56 from Dick Richardson, 40 apiece from Slade and Standen, plus a career best 37 from Len Coldwell, gave Worcestershire a more than handy 60 run lead on first innings. Len Coldwell again was the star with the ball, his 5 – 87 restricted Nottinghamshire to 251 in their second innings, which left the home-side 191 to win.

On the last day it was a case of 'all hands on deck' in mopping up sodden areas following heavy rain, and every spare member of the staff helped, from the Secretary to injured first XI players. This made it possible for the 3,000 spectators to witness Don at his very best, which he had saved until last. The 1963 Club Yearbook described his efforts:

> It was an innings of tremendous power and quality, Kenyon hammered every bowler in every direction with an exhibition of superb stroke play which he can seldom have matched. This was made possible by Graveney's soundness and obvious desire to see his side through and the two of them added an unbeaten 145 for the third wicket in only 104 minutes with Kenyon hitting 18 fours and his partner seven.

Such was the ferocity of Don's innings that W. R. Chignell speculated that 'one wondered how the ball could possibly remain in shape under this onslaught of the boundary rails.' The game was won just before another storm arrived, Don reaching his century with a four that won the match. It was a record fifteenth season that he had completed 1,000 runs for Worcestershire beating the previous best of fourteen by the great Fred Bowley.

As the crowd poured onto the pitch, the Nottinghamshire players applauded the home-side's effort and the champagne corks popped. The only question now was whether Yorkshire could win their game against Glamorgan three days later. Despite losing a day to rain, they secured the requisite win to claim the Championship; Worcestershire had been pipped at the post by just four points.

Graveney, Horton, Richardson and Don all passed 1,000 runs, Don's final figures were 1,399 runs at 25.43 with the two centuries. Len Coldwell was by far away the most successful bowler with 132 wickets (at 18.18) while Flavell, Gifford, Carter and Standen had all claimed well over 50 wickets each. The final word on the 1962 season goes to W. R. Chignell:

> Quietly and undemonstratively Don led the side with dexterity and firmness. The 1961 season had seen his captaincy really blossoming but now it bloomed in profusion and he was obviously the equal of any captain in England. To this could be added a far greater freedom of batting and this was of course, because he knew that he had Tom [Graveney] to come in later.
>
> So Don set about unsettling the enemy attack and this in turn helped Tom. Those who were privileged to see these two great batsmen together in a successful partnership are never likely to forget them.

Chapter 15

After the Lord Mayor's Show and the Rise of One-Day Cricket

As early as March 1963, Don was reticent about the prospects of Worcestershire winning the Championship. In the *Express and Star* he commented, 'Too much has been said by cricket captains in the past few months about how they are going to play and what they are going to do. Anyone who makes a forecast of that nature is sticking his neck out a mile.' He did go as far as stating that Worcestershire might be in contention, but he drew the line there.

On reflection this was wise because the side plummeted to fourteenth in the table and won only four matches all season. While Don passed his customary milestone of 1,000 runs, he reached a hundred just the once. With the exception of Standen, who was not always available due to his football commitments with West Ham United, the side remained the same. W. R. Chignell speculated on the reason for the side's demise and cited the following:

> Kenyon set a good example at the start of the season but the others all had poor seasons for them, and this applied particularly to Richardson and Broadbent. Not even Graveney was in his best form. The fielding was listless and whereas Flavell, Coldwell and Carter took 311 wickets in 1962, they only took 161 in 1963. The problems were compounded because after eight games, Coldwell was injured and remained so for the rest of the season.
>
> On a brighter note, although the spinners Gifford, Slade and Horton made strides forward it was argued that Kenyon could have given them more bowling to do.

Ron Headley made a similar observation:

> The one flaw where I think Don made a mistake was with Doug Slade, as he over protected him. Doug was a superb bowler and would bowl lots of maidens but if you slogged him he couldn't bowl. I saw Don protect him whereas I'd say 'look he's trying to slog you, here's your chance let's set the right field, you are too good to be taken off'. Doug would have been better for that and Giffy could come on if it didn't work.

When *Wisden* was released in April, Don was named one of the Five Cricketers of the Year alongside Mushtaq Mohammad, Peter Parfitt, Phil Sharpe and Fred Titmus.

It noted,

In his fourth year as captain, no other member of the side did more to make it Worcestershire's most glorious and joyous season. Under his skilful guidance and capable handling of the talent at his command the County looked a well-balanced combination. Indeed for Worcestershire to finish runners up for only the second time in sixty-three years of first class cricket was a triumph over adversity and a tribute to Kenyon's leadership.

When I spoke to one of the most respected county and Test captains from the last fifty years, Raymond Illingworth, he commented,

> Don was an excellent player and tactically made very few mistakes. He was also a very good reader of a pitch. As a batsman he was a bloody good player and played Fred very well and would always take him on. Fred felt that as well and would always test him out with a bouncer.
>
> Like Len Hutton he played the off spinner well but they shared a weakness that if it turned they would be beaten through bat and pad. I remember him at Kidderminster in 1956 he scored 200 and plenty and it turned as well. He played Appleyard and Wardle at their best, and we still lost. He had the knack of making everyone look ordinary and I didn't get a bowl until he'd reached 200 so you can imagine how I was feeling!

There were two innovations for the new season, firstly the introduction of the Gillette Cup one-day knockout competition spread over 65 overs. In this, Worcestershire were to reach the first final in September. The second was the introduction of a new front foot rule which Alan Ormrod described to me: 'In 1963 there was the new "no ball system" whereby you had to have the whole foot inside the box and not cutting the line; if you did it was a no ball. This had a big impact on Jack (Flavell) and Bob (Carter) they did not cope with it well. Interestingly it changed again in 1964 to what it is today.'

The opening game with the West Indies was ruined by the rain and the first three championship matches were all drawn. The county was blighted by drawn matches throughout the season, thirteen to be precise, which was nearly 50 per cent of the matches played. During that time Don made a reasonable start with three half-centuries, he was to finish the season with eight more but just the one first class hundred.

In the last week of May, the first Gillette Cup match was played when Surrey were defeated by 114 runs at the Oval. 83 from Headley and 69 from Graveney held the batting together while Jim Standen on one of his rare appearances cleaned up with 5 – 14. Two of the dismissals were caught and bowled which will come as no surprise to many Worcestershire supporters of that era, as Standen was regarded as the best fielder they had seen!

Don's approach to cricket was to attack, and this remained his aim in the new form of the game. This came back to haunt him though in the Gillette Cup Final. Another three consecutive draws followed, the first of which saw Don score 55 in the second innings against Middlesex at Lord's. Over 300 adrift on first innings, the game never looked like being won.

1963, cutting a ball from John Price of Middlesex on the way to 55. © EMPICSPA.

His one and only ton of the season followed at Old Trafford, when in response to Lancashire's 326 – 7 declared, Worcestershire replied with 349 – 4 declared. Don struck 16 fours in a long innings of 166 which saw him become the first ever Worcestershire batsman to score 150 against Lancashire. Headley weighed in with 108 and with just 10 more runs needed for victory, Worcestershire closed on 216 – 6 in a closely fought drawn game.

Every championship game was drawn until the second week of June when Sussex visited New Road; the result was a Sussex victory by 55 runs. Attention was deflected by round two of the Gillette Cup with a visit to Neath to face Glamorgan. Described in the Club's 1964 Yearbook as a magnificent game of cricket, Worcestershire got home by 46 runs thanks to 93 from Graveney. Glamorgan gave them a good run for their money, closing on 192 thanks to 78 from Eiros Lewis. Jeff Jones recalls this game vividly:

It was a very exciting game where Tom was named Man of the Match for his 93. Not many people realise this, but a second award was made by adjudicator, Bill Edrich to Eiros Lewis the off-spinner. He did well and I understand he was presented with a medal too. What I also remember is that about 12,000 people turned up at a club ground, it was packed out. I recall Don being aggressive in one day cricket, he was really in to it; he got his runs quickly especially against the quicks.

Jack Flavell with 5 – 43 from 14 overs, was another worthy man of the match candidate but as Don once said of Graveney: 'He looks a good player even when he's getting out', so how can you compete with that?

Nearly a month to the day since this win, four more draws and two defeats followed before the Gillette Cup semi-final against Lancashire at New Road beckoned. Thanks to one of Flavell's fastest and most hostile spells of bowling, the game was over after only two hours. On a hard wicket he got the ball to lift off a good length and claimed 6 – 14 from 13 overs to rout the visitors for 59 and claim the Man of the Match award. The target of 60 was reached in 11 overs with Don the only casualty to Ken Higgs for 19. To add insult to injury, the home-side won an eighteen over exhibition match as well.

Worcestershire won their first Championship game of the season in mid-July with a 101 run margin over Derbyshire at Buxton in a low scoring game. Graveney with 100 in the first innings came to the rescue along with Flavell who claimed 6 – 46 in the home-side's first innings. Flavell, in the middle of his benefit season, chose the game with Yorkshire as his match. 'Kenyon Shares in Bright Stands with Horton and Headley' was the headline in the *Worcester Evening News* which signalled a return to some sort of form for Don and the other batsmen too. The report also stated, 'On a gloriously sunny morning Kenyon looked well pleased when Flavell began his benefit match by beating Illingworth in the toss. The pitch looked in good condition and success with the coin meant that Flavell would have longer to rest his back.'

Incidentally, Don always used an 1898 Queen Victoria Crown to toss for innings. This coin together with many other items belonging to him are on display in the atrium area of the pavilion at New Road. In reply to Worcestershire's 352 – 7 Yorkshire were dismissed for 166 and 129 to lose by an innings and 57 runs, with the wickets shared.

With Don absent through injury for two of the next three games, which were all defeats, by late August, Worcestershire were languishing in fifteenth place in the championship. Back to back wins against Northamptonshire and Somerset helped ease the situation with Don scoring a polished 60 in the second game. The miserable Championship season finished with one further draw and one further defeat. During my research I spoke with journalist Mike Beddow, an ever present in the press box at New Road who recalled his first meeting with Don:

> It was a helping hand from Don Kenyon that eased my introduction to cricket reporting in general and in particular chronicling the year-by-year fortunes of Worcestershire for half-a-century. I first met Don in August 1963. The county were playing Gloucestershire at the College Ground and it was not one of the warmest or sunniest of Cheltenham Festivals. Don was writing a column in the *Sports Argus*, and while I was at the match, representing The *Birmingham Post*, I had a call from the editor of the Saturday night sports paper, asking if I could help them by getting a few words from the skipper. Totally new to the environment of cricket reporting – a slightly reticent twenty-two year old who was more used to working at football grounds – I picked my moment to tap on the dressing room door. 'Someone to see you, Skipper,' said the attendant. In I went, nervously

looking round the room. Tom Graveney over there, Ronnie Headley next to me, Martin Horton in the corner. In fact I was walking into a group who would all be County Champions in the following summer. A friendly voice, recognisable to anyone familiar with Stourbridge and the wider Black Country, welcomed me in.

Straightaway Don put the apprentice ghost-writer at ease, delivering all the words I needed to fill the space allocated in *The Argus*. I thought of that day again last year when I had the good fortune to celebrate my 50th anniversary at New Road. It was partly with Don Kenyon's help that I set out on a lifetime in cricket Press Boxes, not only at New Road but all around the county circuit.

Lord's was now the venue for the first ever Gillette Cup Final where Worcestershire were to play Sussex. In Gordon Ross' *The Gillette Cup 1963 – 1980,* Sussex captain Ted Dexter wrote,

> Sussex won that final much against the run of play, but at least the game was being taken seriously by that stage of the season. Earlier it had been treated with a cross between mild amusement and palpable disdain by some of the old school players, which showed them up for having an odd sense of humour at best and, at worst, a basic misunderstanding of the history and origins of cricket.

Similar statements were trotted out in 2003 when Twenty-20 cricket was first introduced and, like the Gillette Cup used to be, has become the centrepiece of the cricket season in under a decade since its inception. Like it or not, we must accept that the game is forever evolving.

In the *Sunday Telegraph* for 8 September, Michael Melford's headline summed up the game: 'It's Agony as Sussex just Pip Worcester'. 'Worcestershire were beaten just before seven o'clock in the 64th over after Booth and Carter had added 21 runs amid great excitement for the last wicket.' Man of the Match Gifford had earlier broken the back of the Sussex innings by claiming 4 – 33 from his 15 overs, which restricted Sussex to 168. A steady loss of wickets from Worcestershire, however, put them behind almost from the word go. The County lost the first Lord's final by 14 runs. Dexter's captaincy came in for criticism in *Wisden*, which reported at being unhappy that he had placed the entire field around the boundary to prevent rapid scoring. It was this tactical nous which got the better of Don on the day due to his desire to continue to attack whenever he could.

In the *Evening Mail* Peter Bryan's article 'Kenyon Hits at Dexter Tactics' revealed more about the final: 'Worcestershire captain Don Kenyon today dismissed Dexter's tactics with one word … sacrilege.' He continued, 'We should have won, we did not take enough quick singles and we did not bat very well. The tactics of putting all the fielders on the boundary are ruining the game. It is a waste of time playing it'. Strong words from Don, but this was another indication of how the game was changing as it was entering a new professional era. E. W. 'Jim' Swanton provided a crumb of comfort by praising Worcestershire's well balanced approach. He was referring to the three spinners included in the side whereas Sussex had played all of their games with an all seam attack. In the final analysis, however, one cannot take away the fact that Sussex won!

In August 2014 I received a brief e-mail from Ted Dexter following my request for his comments on Don:

> Hardly knew the guy; previous era. Only quote I have in mind concerns a favourable report of a young bowler – 'just bring him down to Worcester and we'll soon see how good he is.' Batted with him for a short while in a Test at Old Trafford, he kept calling me for impossible short singles and then throwing up his hands as if it were my fault.

While it does not reveal a great deal, I'm left wondering if there is something 'unsaid' which remains within his comments or indeed there is 'no love lost' between them?

The 1963 Gillette Cup Final was a disappointing conclusion to a disappointing season. Don had scored 1,393 runs at 35.13 with just the one hundred which was not to his usual high standard. Four other batsmen passed the 1,000 mark yet no bowler claimed 100 wickets, only Flavell with eighty-three came close. 1964, therefore, needed to be another season of improvement following this setback.

Chapter 16

Champions

In *Tom Graveney: The Biography*, by Christopher Sandford, Graveney commented on Worcestershire's success in 1964,

> Many factors contribute to the production of a side that wins the County Championship, we were a very well balanced side and nearly every time we had to call on a reserve, it proved to be successful. Without doubt we were wonderfully led by Don Kenyon. Right from the word go Don proved what I had always thought him to be: a steady, solid and unworried character. Even in the more tense situations, Don remained Don. He was calm and unruffled in the bad spell when we lost three matches out of four. Don maintained that we were not to be put off by defeat, providing we were beaten going for victory. Events proved him completely right.

As the season was about to start the *Worcester Evening News* reported in April that 'County players go automatic' which was a reference to four Ford cars which had been loaned for the use of the team during the season; however, it was not without incident. Alan Ormrod said,

> What made Don angry was if you misbehaved or did anything which embarrassed the club. We used to go round in a bus at one time but after that we got cars. The first time we drove to London one of the players was locked up for speeding, (I think) I can't recall if he was drunk as well but it was before drink driving. Don had to go to the police station and get him out, he wasn't too happy about that! If he wasn't happy, you'd just look at his eyes, his eyes emphasised what he was trying to get across, you could feel what he was expressing. Sometimes this expression would tell you, plain and simple, that you were a bloody idiot.

Speaking at Stourbridge Cricket Society in April 2014, Bob Carter said how Don would also get his message across. Bob Carter recalled, 'It was simple, he would either put his arm around you or place his hands on his hips and say "what are you? You are a professional and you know what you are doing." There was no loss of temper; a quiet word is all that it took; a brilliant man manager.'

1964 was Don's testimonial year. On the pitch, an early exit to Glamorgan in the Gillette Cup allowed Worcestershire to place every effort into the Championship but not until a draw was first played out against Bob Simpson's

Australians. The highlight was the return of a fully fit Len Coldwell who claimed 7 – 53. Don batted at number four to allow Richardson and Horton to open and making his first class debut at number seven was Basil D'Oliveira. He was qualifying with Kidderminster in the Birmingham League during the season and was, therefore, unavailable for selection in the Championship.

Four straight victories over Lancashire, Middlesex, Glamorgan and Leicestershire got the campaign off to a flying start, Don's best in that time was 50 in the innings and 81 run victory over Glamorgan but in two of the four games Coldwell had taken 7 – 25 and 7 – 44 which equated to a wicket every thirty-five deliveries while Norman Gifford chipped in with 7 – 31 against Leicestershire. The game at Leicestershire was a prime example of Don's reading of the game. He gambled by declaring and setting the home-side a target of just 149, a target they fell 44 runs short of thanks to Gifford. As Tom Graveney put it: 'No team that wins the Championship does so without taking risks and this one paid off for Don.'

Don's and Worcestershire's first century of the season came at New Road in the rain-affected drawn-game, with Yorkshire. The *Worcester Evening News* stated, 'Kenyon first ton up boy'. 'Kenyon cheered a New Road crowd of well over 3,000 watching in miserable weather by moving to his 100 with his twelfth four in just over four hours.'

Ron Headley, with 117 plus six wickets apiece from Carter (6 – 45) and Flavell (6 – 28), saw Worcestershire beat Kent at Dartford by the impressive margin of 230 runs. Despite hundreds from Horton (116) and Richardson (103) a second draw of the season followed in another rain interrupted game against Sussex. The form of the home-side had captured the public's imagination because 8,000 people crammed into New Road for the Sussex game. Don's comment some years earlier about the need to play attractive cricket in order to encourage more spectators to watch was never more pertinent.

Another win in a cliff-hanger at Chesterfield was achieved thanks once more to a declaration at the start of the final day with Worcestershire still 113 runs in arrears on first innings. Fair play to Derbyshire, they set the visitors 174 to win in even time which they duly did thanks to a last wicket partnership between Gifford and Carter who hit the winning runs off the penultimate ball of the game just as it started to rain once more.

'Standen Snaps 7 – 35' was the headline in the *Daily Mail* in early June, as Jim helped roll over Glamorgan for just 71 at the Arms Park in Cardiff, with the *Birmingham Post's* headline: 'White flag Comes Out for Kenyon' making interesting reading. It quoted, 'A white flag was hung from the dressing rooms at Cardiff yesterday in jocular token of surrender to Don Kenyon who had just sent a six hurtling through the window with the speed of a rocket.' Set 109 they romped home by nine wickets with Don being dismissed for a typically pugnacious 49.

Two drawn games against Surrey and fellow table toppers Warwickshire left both sides neck and neck with seventy-two points each, twice the number of the team in third place; it was fast becoming a two horse race as early as the middle of June. 60 and 92 in the second innings against each opponent was a good return for Don as the *Birmingham Post* bragged: 'Midlands Top – Rest Nowhere.' The other good news was that a record breaking crowd of 13,000 attended the first day's play against Warwickshire at New Road, the most seen inside the ground since Bradman's Australians visited in 1948. Although the Warwickshire game had ended in a draw, it had strengthened Worcestershire's points tally thanks to Jack Flavell. The *Daily Express* described the game as 'a table top thriller' and ran the headline: 'Flavell by One Run – Jack's Rocket Wrecks 'Em.' This was reference to Flavell who snatched two first innings points (for a first innings lead) by, as the report said, 'flattening the leg stump of Ron Miller with the fastest ball of the day.' Len Coldwell said at the time that he had never heard a roar like it and even Jim Sanden who had played in the FA Cup Final was shaken sitting in the pavilion as twelfth man.

Don, however, found himself having to defend his position a few days later in the *Daily Mail*. Kenyon had set Warwickshire 243 runs in 75 minutes and apologised for that: 'It was a great pity the match had to end this way but what else could I do? Our plans went wrong in the first hour when we lost three quick wickets. Mike Smith, Warwickshire's captain fully understood my position and we acknowledged that it was impossible to stage a phoney finish in a match as important as this.'

The good form continued with a 122 run victory against Somerset at the Imperial Tobacco Ground in Bristol thanks to another unsung hero, Brian Brain who claimed match figures of 10 – 166 and was playing due to Flavell, Gifford and Coldwell being away on Test duty. It was the mark of a good side that could produce another win with three key players absent. A low-scoring game at Derby followed, in which Worcestershire edged home by 43 runs with all the wickets being shared by the seamers.

In another low-scoring encounter at Edgbaston, Worcestershire claimed an invaluable win in this return fixture. In reply to Worcestershire's 119, Warwickshire were humbled for 72 with Standen claiming 6 – 45 and thanks to a partnership of 124 between Headley (78) and Graveney (95), the visitors declared at 258 – 8 to set the home-side 306 for victory.

The *Birmingham Post* had speculated: 'Will Don Kenyon go flat out for victory?' This question was answered when Warwickshire were dismissed for 86 in their second innings with three wickets apiece for Coldwell, Gifford and Horton with the last five wickets tumbling for just 25 runs. Kenyon's side were now outright leaders with the *Daily Express* proclaiming, 'Worcester whiz-bangs race ahead' while Keith Miller wrote, 'Kenyon's men tame pitch.' This second headline was a reference to the technically skilled batting of Headley and Graveney which drew praise from the great Australian. He went on record as saying, 'In front of 20,000 spectators, this is the best county match I have seen in years.'

The first defeat of the season came at New Road against Somerset who deservedly won by 83 runs thanks to a dogged 100 not out by Roy Virgin out of Somerset's second innings total of 195 – 8; it was the difference between the sides.

During this game, Eric Cooper of the *Daily Express* wrote a feature on Don: 'A quiet man with 1,000 innings in the book.' He wrote, 'Don Kenyon, a man rarely touched by cricket's glamour but endowed with all the games' graces is set for quite a year. The forty-year-old batsman skipper has now topped 1,000 innings in first class cricket and is one of a mere thirty-six English batsmen to have scored more than 30,000 first class runs.'

A draw at Dudley against Essex drew the most unusual and rare headline in the *Daily Mail* on 21 July: 'Kenyon Bags First Pair for Sixteen Years'. Barry Knight 'did for him' in each innings and claimed 11 – 142 in the match.

Thankfully two defeats against Yorkshire at Scarborough and Hampshire at New Road proved to be nothing more than a minor setback in the run in to the end of the season. 109 from Graveney helped to secure an innings and 27 run victory over Leicestershire while Norman Gifford's match return was 10 – 87.

In early August, Tom Duckworth in the *Sports Argus* wrote an article in which he questioned whether Duncan Fearnley was ready to move up to open the innings with Don dropping himself to number five? He said,

> I understand that Kenyon has long been turning over this question in his mind. Now, following recent experiences, he is coming to the decision that the switch would be in Worcestershire's interests and his own. The strain, both mental and physical, of captaining the side and also of opening the batting is a heavy one, particularly at the end of the day. Consequently he is often unable to do himself justice as a batsman.

A similar experiment had not worked in 1961 and these words of caution were to prove premature just a few weeks later. Although the next game with Northamptonshire was drawn, special mention must be reserved for Tom Graveney who completed his 100th first class hundred in the game with a first innings 132. Tom and Don had first become firm friends on the tour to India and Pakistan during 1951/52 despite it being a difficult six months because of Don's homesickness. Their friendship extended to opening a sports shop in Redditch which they co-owned, it later became Graveney Sports in its own right.

A second consecutive hundred for Graveney followed (106) in the first innings against Essex at Leyton while Dick Richardson made an unbeaten 117 in the second innings to help Worcestershire get back on track with a 167 run victory. Flavell with 5 – 75 and 4 – 58 was the pick of the bowlers. A thrilling one wicket victory followed at Trent Bridge where Worcestershire were set 168 to win. Flavell had been the hero with 6 – 67 in the first innings and splendidly he proved to be the hero once more, but this time with the bat.

At 135 – 7 it looked a lost cause, with the tension getting to the players. Some of them went to the back of the pavilion unable to watch, while Graveney went to his car in an attempt to complete the crossword just to take his mind off things. With 9 down and still 9 needed for victory, Carter joined Flavell in the middle then Flavell struck Keith Gillhouley for 2 fours to win the game and keep Worcestershire on top.

An encouraging 91 from Don in the second innings at Cheltenham was the difference in helping Worcestershire to declare at 281 – 4 with both sides being dismissed for 143 in the first innings. Flavell with 10 – 110 was yet again the best of the bowlers with Brain backing him up with match figures of 6 – 71. In all it resulted in a victory by 107 runs. 'Kenyon Spurs Worcestershire' was the headline which also celebrated 'the emergence of Don Kenyon from a run of low scores' which could not have been timed better. 'John's Nine Sets Pace in Thriller' was the headline in the *Daily Mirror* when Worcestershire met Middlesex at Kidderminster. Yet again, Flavell had given his team a stranglehold with 9 – 56 from 25 overs but in spite of this, the home-side only managed a narrow first innings lead. In their second innings, Middlesex were dismissed for just 112, described as 'pathetic batting' in Worcestershire's 1965 Yearbook, which meant Worcestershire needed 108 for victory.

An improving Kenyon, along with Horton, attacked from the off with the first 50 coming up in 57 minutes and the second 50 in 98 minutes. Don finished on 53 not out to help secure a nine wicket victory at 6.20 p.m. on the second evening. 'Kenyon Hustle Smashes Jitters' was the headline in the *Express and Star* where it stated that he 'battered spinners Titmus and Drybrough into the railway alongside the ground, and spangled 9 fours.' He was running into form at precisely the right time.

As Andrew Hignell wrote in his excellent book, *Summer of '64*, this result also meant that Worcestershire would become County Champions if they recorded another victory in the following match against Gloucestershire at Worcester and Warwickshire failed to win against Hampshire at Southampton. On the morning of the game hundreds of spectators flooded into the ground in the hope of seeing history made. If there had been any nerves they soon disappeared as Don won the toss and batted. In a brisk and purposeful start the *Evening News* later reported, 'Kenyon and Horton in 187 Runs Stand'. It read: 'A crowd of 5,000 saw the opening batsmen in a three and a half hour partnership, the County's biggest of the summer. Kenyon who hammered 91 at Cheltenham on Monday, did even better today scoring 114, his second century this term.'

With Horton dismissed for 96, Headley (103 not out) and Graveney (57) helped put on 126 for the third wicket. Headley showed a liking for the Ladies' Pavilion pulling 2 tremendous sixes into the enclosure and moved from 62 to 96 in just 15 minutes. It allowed the home skipper to declare at 398 – 3. Weekend rain freshened the wicket and with Flavell claiming 3 – 9 in the space of 4 overs, the visitors were in trouble. Despite some resistance from the tail they were dismissed for 192 with Gifford claiming 3 – 61. Following on, Gloucestershire struggled to 77 – 6 but a dogged 68 from David Allen stopped the rot. Gifford continued to chip away until the last pair were at the wicket.

Tom Graveney said, 'My brother Ken played in this last game. He said, "I'm not coming out to bloody field again", so told Roy (Booth) to get ready and was stumped. Roy did the rest as Ken walked down the wicket and we had won; not just by an innings and two runs margin but maybe the title as well.' While congratulations poured in, the celebrations were on hold until the result from Southampton, where Warwickshire needing a win to prolong the Championship race, were acquitting themselves well. As the game entered the last quarter of an hour they needed 26 more runs to win with just two wickets in hand. Just an hour and three quarters after Worcestershire had seen off Gloucestershire, news came through that Derek Shackleton and 'Butch' White had taken the two wickets to inflict a defeat over Warwickshire and so the celebrations could begin; Worcestershire had won the title with three matches still to play.

The celebrations were tempered with the knowledge that the players had to travel to Eastbourne for the next match against Sussex. Before departing, Don was able to pose for a favourite picture from his own archive, taken with Jean and daughters Sue and Lesley.

The Times paid tribute to 'Kenyon's mature leadership' while the *Birmingham Post* summed up the season beautifully: 'A flying start – and Don Kenyon's men never looked back.'

Although the game at Eastbourne was drawn, it was a personal triumph for Don as the *Daily Express* reported, 'Majestic Kenyon Leads Slam'. Crawford White wrote, 'Skipper Don Kenyon celebrated Worcester's new status as champs with a majestic, unbeaten 158. "It couldn't have been at a better place", grinned the Don, still savouring the achievement 24 hours later. I'm a bit partial to this ground, I've had hundreds in my last three knocks here and this is my third century and highest of the season.' Some years later Don recalled,

> We had travelled to Eastbourne after a good party, our families came along too. Eastbourne is such a beautiful part of the south coast, it meant they could be part of the celebrations as well. Arriving a little jaded, we did well because we bowled Sussex out for 279 and I had to bat towards the close of day one.
>
> I wasn't one to live it up and was sober when I went out to bat but the innings gave me great pleasure due to the fact I batted five and a half hours for 158 not out, we had won the Championship for the first time and the boys were so happy.

Celebrating '64 style. © Mirrorpix.

With Jean
and daughters
Lesley and Sue.
© Berrows
Newspapers.

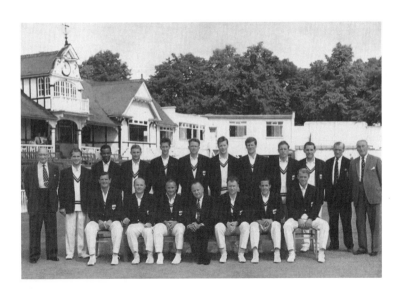

1964 County
Champions.
From the
Kenyon family
collection.

To cap it all, Don's testimonial fund had raised £6,351, seven years after his benefit. The season closed with two more victories, a ten-wicket hammering of Nottinghamshire and a 73-run margin over Lancashire, both games being played at Worcester. The last game was skippered by Martin Horton; Don had been laid low with a throat infection. Don's figures for the season were 1,480 runs at 29.60 with the three hundreds, while four other batsmen – Graveney, Headley, Horton and Richardson – also scored 1,000 runs, while Flavell and Gifford topped 100 wickets. 1964 really had been a season to remember!

Chapter 17

Celebrating Success, Taking on the World and the Championship Retained in the Centenary Year

On 23 September 1964 a lavish dinner was held at Barneshall Restaurant in Worcester to celebrate winning the Championship. Don provided the response to 'Gubby' Allen and in true fashion he had prepared in meticulous detail.

Among Don's personal papers is the exact speech he wrote, something Jean said he prepared many weeks in advance and kept changing. From the annotations he made it's easy to understand her view. Written in long hand on Dudley Iron and Steel note paper, Don's name is quoted as one of the company representatives, as is Eric Hollies the great Warwickshire player. Cleverly it states, 'Don't STEEL this pad, use it for your notes'. Don pays tribute to players from down the ages and is mindful to recognise the contribution which those behind the scenes made, from the scorer Bill Faithfull to the dressing room attendant, Ernie Stocker and to Mike Biddle the groundsman. The speech ran to eleven pages in total, and Don closes by stating:

> I think we must now look to the future and next year. We shall have Basil D'Oliveira qualified and barring injuries and loss of form there is no reason why we shouldn't have a successful a year as we have enjoyed this. And of course if this is the case we shall all be looking forward to the continued support of our supporters which has been one of the features of our cricket at New Road during the past few years.

Earlier in the month the *Birmingham Post* ran a story saying that 'Kenyon wants to show flag to world.' At a cocktail party hosted by the Mayor and Mayoress of Worcester, he said, 'There was nothing the team would like more than to be able to show the Championship pennant to as many parts of the world as possible.' The idea came to fruition in February.

As preparations were underway, Don continued to hit the headlines for all the right reasons. In November, the *Kidderminster Times* ran a heart-warming story about eleven-year-old Robert Davies, who was injured in a car crash and lost his voice as a result. When he did speak again the first words he managed to speak were 'Kenyon' and 'Talbot'. These were references to his two heroes, Don and Tony Talbot a cricketer with local side Chaddesley Corbett. When Tony heard of this, he rang Don to see if he would pay a visit to Robert to help aid his recovery, to which he agreed. Don promised that he would also introduce the youngster to the rest of the team which he duly did during a hockey match between the Worcestershire cricketers and Kidderminster Hockey Club.

The other good piece of news was that Don was named as Cricketer of the Year by the Lord's Taverners. Reported in the local *Express and Star*, the news also filtered as far as the *Toowoomba Chronicle* in Australia. On 14 January 1965 it reported, 'The Cricketer of the Year award goes to Don Kenyon who led his county to the Championship this season. As a county cricketer he has a brilliant record and his ability to mould an average set of cricketers into a winning combination has won him the coveted award.' Details of the world tour emerged in the *Evening News* on 11 February with the impressive headline: 'Across the World with Worcestershire'. They planned to play 14 games in eight weeks which would help to get the celebrations of the Club's centenary well and truly underway. Some 34,000 miles taking in seven different countries would be made, quite an itinerary for twelve players and the manager Joe Lister.

On the eve of departure, the players gathered for a celebration dinner at The Worcester Guildhall hosted by the Supporters' Association in recognition of the previous season's achievements. Don commented in the *Worcester Evening News* on the prospects for 1965: 'We must have the run of the ball to keep the Championship. We had it a number of times last season and this, with other little items adds up to being champions.' He also had one desire for the upcoming tour and set out with one aim – to get the world interested in cricket – and, as Martin Horton said in an interview in 2004, 'We did exactly that.'

Arriving in Nairobi and heading straight into a press conference, Don was quoted by the *East African Standard*, 'Worcestershire promise attacking cricket.' The captain commented, 'This game will, I am sure, be a close one to watch and we must keep the game alive both for the spectators and the players. I will be careful not to over-bowl my bowlers as they have two months of continuous bowling to do before they get back to England.' Being 'his own man', there was no rest, he ordered nets prior to the three day game, he was taking nothing for granted. In a drawn game, he was dismissed for 82 with D'Oliveira starring with a typically hard hit 162 while Graveney chipped in with 92. Don commented, 'Basil got us out of trouble with a brilliant knock; it's good that he and Tom both have experience of playing on jute matting.'

In his 1968 book, *D'Oliveira: An Autobiography*, Basil commented on his approach to playing for his new county:

> I stayed in the nets at Worcester until my roots went down deeper than the grass. Constantly I kept an eye on Kenyon and Graveney, particularly on Kenyon when he was playing the quick bowlers, not simply because of his movement of the back foot which I was already in the process of stealing from him, but because his record against the quicks was so good that practically everything was of interest. My general methods were heading in the direction of his. Not so polished, not so effective, but basically similar.

The first-class fixture in Bulawayo was hard fought with the captain adding 63 in the second innings. Len Brown in the *Bulawayo Chronicle* reported that 'Kenyon's was the only innings of note. Slightly on the subdued side, he

Batting against Kenya Cricket Association, February 1965. From the Kenyon family collection.

nevertheless played some glorious drives, both through the covers and to the outfield over the fielders' heads.'

Thanks to 5 – 18 and 5 – 26 from Len Coldwell, the champions got home by 196 runs with Len Brown waxing lyrical about Coldwell's performance describing him and Flavell as, 'the finest seamers we've seen here in years.' Rhodesia were to have their revenge in a 167-run victory ten days later which followed the drawn game at Que Que where Headley stroked a highly attractive 178.

In the souvenir brochure Basil Bray, Chairman of the Que Que Sports Club welcomed the visitors: 'We are particularly pleased to welcome Don Kenyon back to Que Que where in 1951 he spent a short time coaching local aspirants of the game. These have watched his career with interest and join all of us at the Sports Club in congratulating him and his team on winning their first County Championship.'

During their stay in Que Que, the players attended a dinner on 25 February at the Sebakwe Hotel. The menu was presented in the most original of ways as a special tribute to the guests:

Stuffed Eggs Worcestershire
***

Cream of Que Que Asparagus
Cold Consommé Coldwell
***

Fried Kingklip Kenyon and Maxwell Sauce
***

Spaghetti Italienne in D'Oliveira Oil
Baked Rhodesian Gammon with Graveney Sauce
***

Roast Sirloin of Beef and Horton Horseradish Sauce
Roast Stuffed Slade Chicken with Brain Sauce
***

Vegetables from Gifford Gardener
Flavell, Lister and Matkin Potatoes
***

Championship Pudding

Tea plantation presentation in Calcutta, 5–6 March 1965. From the Kenyon family collection.

(Rich)ardson Brandy Sauce
***
Ice Cream
Really Coldwell Encore
***
Headley Cheese and Biscuits
***
Tea or Coffee OR Booth

The next leg of the tour saw a stop-off in Calcutta where two games were drawn with Graveney (104), D'Oliveira (104) and Headley (102) in prime form. During the game at the Ballygunge Ground, the players were presented with a supply of tea to commemorate the visit; no doubt one of the more unusual presentations associated with cricket.

A disappointing single was Don's only contribution to the game against Malaysia (played in Singapore) where 161 from Graveney rescued the County who wrapped up a win by 148 runs thanks to 7 – 31 from D'Oliveira in the first Malaysian innings and 7 – 38 from Gifford in the second. Two more draws followed, one against Singapore and the other against the Selangor State XI in Kuala Lumpur. In the return game with Malaysia, Don chipped in with 54 as the visitors cruised to an innings and 117 runs victory.

The players were also greeted with the news in the *Daily Mail* that Don had been appointed as an England selector for the first time. In a meeting held at Lord's, Club chairman Gilbert Ashton and acting Secretary, Arthur Ross-Slater represented Worcestershire's case to have Kenyon appointed to the panel. It meant that the champion county would be without Don's services for at least five matches, because as a selector he was required to attend at least one day of each Test match with the exception of the last. England were to have a six Test

Left: Outside the Old Supreme Court Building in Singapore opposite the Pedang, 13–15 March 1965. From the Kenyon family collection.

Below: On the tarmac at Honolulu, 30 March 1965. From the Kenyon family collection.

summer playing three matches against both New Zealand and South Africa.

In Bangkok, against the Royal Bangkok Sports Club a victory by 180 runs was achieved thanks to 117 from D'Oliveira and 5 – 24 from Coldwell. The same margin of victory followed against the Hong Kong Cricket League President's XI thanks to Graveney's 116. Once again, Graveney starred with 132 as an innings and 101 run victory was wrapped up against Hong Kong in Kowloon on 27 March.

A six-hour delay en route to the next stopover, Honolulu, did not help matters. The intriguing aspect of this leg of the tour was an interview which Don did with Hal Wood, the sports editor of the *Honolulu Advertiser*. He began with an insight into how he viewed the game: 'More fans turn out to watch a marble game than showed up to witness the great Worcestershire County Cricket Club, champions of all England.

This guy Graveney can hit the ball in cricket like Mantle or Willie Mays in baseball ... out of the park.' He talked to Don referring to him as a 'splendid chap really', one imagines delivered almost with an air of surprise.

Don Kenyon said, 'This Graveney is a great one, one of the really greats. He has played in fifty Test matches during the past fifteen years.' Hal Wood went on to quantify this, 'A Test is one in which an all-star British team is chosen to meet a club from Australia, Pakistan, India or some other country. To be chosen is like being made an All-American for fifteen years in a row; that's Graveney.' Don also explained, 'Cricket, however, is a losing proposition. The total payroll for a Club may be around $58,000 for a season. We play to average crowds of about 8,000 and for big Test matches the crowds may run as high as 45,000.' The game produced a comfortable win for Worcestershire by 136 runs with the home-side being dismissed for 48, thanks to three wickets apiece from Gifford and D'Oliveira. The tour ended on a disappointing note with the game scheduled against the South Californian Cricket Association at Hollywood being cancelled due to rain.

On his return home, Don had bought an array of gifts for the family. Thorough to say the least, he kept the receipts for every item he bought, this being another example of his attention to detail, an approach he took in to planning every aspect of his life. Strings of pearls, clothing, pendants, coin purses, paper weights and silk fans were just some of the items purchased. Despite being regarded as 'tight with money' by some, this is a prime example of him ploughing every effort and every available pound of his money into making the best possible life for his loved ones.

His daughter, Sue Jackson, remembers him coming home:

We skived off school so that we could see him; it seemed as if he had been away forever. On this tour he wrote back and sent postcards from many of the destinations.

He got less homesick as he got older I think he became more accepting of it. Dad was like Dan (Sue's son Daniel) in so many ways, a Taurus – home birds ... an earth sign of feeling comfortable in a rut. They have no desire to climb out and see what it's like. If we went away, he'd want to go back to the same restaurant the next evening. His attitude was we have been here before, why change?

Yes, he was very much a creature of habit, probably comfortable in the company of his own team but less so with people he didn't know so well, even though he would know them from various county games. Definitely, he was his own man.'

In the 1965 Gillette Cup a first round exit to Sussex did not bode well, and in the Championship, the team had to wait until the sixth match before they tasted victory. This was a 251 run hammering of Lancashire at New Road thanks to a second innings haul of 6 – 7 in an amazing spell from Bob Carter. Captain for this game Tom Graveney had opened his run scoring for the season with a majestic 104 while Basil D'Oliveria had exploded onto the scene with hundreds (106 and 163) in the back to back fixtures against Essex.

Graveney's form posed a dilemma for his Captain/Selector and that was to decide whether he was worthy of a place in the England side or whether (to the delight of the Worcestershire fans) he left him out and risk being accused of bias. The *Birmingham Post's* article, 'Graveney Poser for Selector Kenyon', said as much. It proved though to be no more than speculation, Graveney was not selected for either series. A draw against Nottinghamshire and a defeat to Kent at Dartford in Don's next two games meant that in twelve championship innings he had mustered just 213 runs. Already he had encountered a stop/start to the campaign having to miss three games because of his selector's duties.

Don echoed this disappointment in an article for the *Sports Argus* where he said, 'Even when you are in the lower half of the table struggling to get going, it's still tough being Champions. I don't want to make any excuses we have been giving some bad performances. In short, we are not clicking.' In an attempt to rediscover some form, Don dropped himself to six in the order for the eight wicket victory over Derbyshire, although personally the move only yielded 8 runs for him.

It was now 8 June and Don still had not hit a 50. Matters were made worse because he was not to play again until later in the month in the Championship game against Gloucestershire. On 10 June a welcome distraction was the staging of the Centenary Match between Worcestershire and the MCC at New Road. The visitors' side contained ten internationals, with Denis Compton stealing the limelight with a typically charismatic 75, however their score of 200 was 61 runs short of the target set by Worcestershire. Batting at number six once more, Don contributed 11 not out and he would have to miss the five wicket defeat by Middlesex a week later.

In the next four games Don's return was just 47 runs from seven innings during which time three games were drawn and one, against Somerset, was lost by an innings and 5 runs. The bowling was holding up well with Flavell being in tremendous touch with 7 – 40 against Lancashire, 6 – 31 against Derbyshire and 7 – 54 against Somerset keeping him at the forefront of the leading wicket takers. With Don away on Test duty a welcome six wicket victory against Glamorgan was recorded with Flavell 6 – 56 and half-centuries from D'Oliveira and Graveney helping Worcestershire get over the line. Don remained absent for the next four games, with the last one yielding another win following one abandonment and two draws.

Kent were on the receiving end of a nine wicket thumping with D'Oliveira hitting 107 which contained a six and 16 fours. With the bowlers sharing the wickets this proved one of the most satisfying outcomes of the season to date. It also proved to be the turning point in what had up until now been disappointing to say the least

The key thing for Worcestershire was that Don was now available for nine out of the ten remaining games. A second pivotal moment was described by Ron Headley:

> Club President Sir George Dowty was a winner, half way through the season we came back from an away match and he called us into the committee room. He said that he always managed by incentive and as a winner himself; he wanted us to win the Championship. He reassured us that he knew we would give it our best shot and confirmed that as he would do in business, he would make the incentive worthwhile. It was a lot of money, but we came out and won eight out of the last nine matches to clinch the title once more.

The fight back began with an eight wicket victory over Sussex at Worcester in what was a very low scoring game with Graveney's 63 not out being the only contribution over fifty on either side. Don, still batting down the order at number six was bowled by John Snow without score.

Tom Duckworth in the *Sports Argus* picked up on the shift in momentum with the headline: 'Champion Form Worcestershire' as Derbyshire were dismissed for just 80 and 68 in the next game, with Coldwell turning in a blistering spell of 4 – 7 and D'Oliveira 4 – 26. Gifford, with 7 – 23 in the second innings, ensured that Worcestershire's total of 179 was still enough to inflict and innings and 31 run defeat on the home-side.

Don was not complimentary about the pitch in the drawn encounter with Hampshire at New Road. Commenting in the *Birmingham Post*, he stated that the pitch was docile and 'we would have a job bowling out a girls' school team on it.' Despite this, a ten wicket match haul from Flavell, nearly helped to pull off an unlikely victory. Set 157 in a shade over two hours, the visitors hung on and closed at 77 – 8 to save the game.

The *Worcester Evening News* had already dismissed chances of the title being retained with the headline: 'Missed Catches put Worcestershire out of the Running.' It went on to state, 'The Champions have lost ground which they cannot now reasonably hope to regain.' The captain, on the other hand, wrote in the *Sports Argus*: 'We have that old title feeling again. With the title fight now wide open between half a dozen teams, we are in with a real and a very good chance. Some of our players are re-gaining form and confidence and we feel that we have hit form at the right time.'

Leicestershire were humbled by an innings and 225 runs at New Road with Flavell, Coldwell and D'Oliveira sharing the wickets. Only 5 overs of spin were bowled by Gifford across the two innings. Hundreds from Graveney and D'Oliveira were the outstanding performances, however Don did strike his first half-century of the season (51) which he did 'with some style' according to the write up in the Club's 1966 Yearbook.

The tide had now well and truly turned and Worcestershire were racing back up the table. Gloucestershire lost by seven wickets at Cheltenham thanks to fifties in each innings from D'Oliveira. D'Oliveira was having an outstanding first season, Ron Headley paid tribute to the way his captain managed him:

Bas was a very fit player he used to run up and down the hills in South Africa. When he came to England part of the culture was when the game finished, you had a drink; it didn't take much to get him going. Bas played his first season under a lot of pressure driven by a desire to succeed and Don recognised it.

Somehow, Don seemed to know if Bas had come in at two or three in the morning, and he would ask him to have a bowl. On a boiling hot day he'd keep him on for two hours; he wouldn't come off, or bowl a couple of bad overs but because of his character he'd keep going.

I've seen him bowl from the first ball of the morning until lunch, but he would keep it tight. After lunch, he went to third man but Don had him on again; he'd ask 'where are you going Bas?' This was outstanding man management from Don he knew each individual ... and they knew him. He was a stable, solid and individual man.

If ever a captain's knock was needed, it came in the nine wicket victory over Somerset at Kidderminster. Flavell with match figures of 13 – 96 and Coldwell with 7 – 104 destroyed Somerset in a low scoring game. 'Saucy Worcester' was the headline in the *Sports Argus* which heralded a return to Don's best form of the season. Needing 129 to win, Kenyon was the hero crashing 3 sixes and 12 fours in an innings of 77, by far his best contribution of the season and sharing with Headley, the only century opening stand that year.

In spite of the captain 'bagging a pair' against closest rivals Northamptonshire, a seven wicket victory followed, which proved to be crucial in the knowledge that Worcestershire had denied them any points. Sadly Don's miserable run continued with a third duck in a row this time against Surrey at New Road. Once more the headline in the *Worcester Evening News* highlighted the outstanding performance of the bowlers: 'Coldwell Crashes Through Surrey' and with figures of 8 – 38 from 21 overs, it's plain to see why. Gifford with 6 – 33 in the second innings helped continue the winning habit by an innings and 92.

The penultimate game at Bournemouth was a cracker for so many reasons. Batting first, the visitors declared at 363 – 9 with Ron Hedley again recalling another of his vivid memories of the season:

> Everyone was showing nerves in a different way so Don breezed in and said 'right you bastards what are we going to do today? If I win the toss what should I do? ... We've got a range of opinions.' But as he stood there saying all of this it had broken any remaining tension. He went on to say 'It's alright for you, I've got to make a decision', but you knew he'd always make up his own mind.
>
> He then called me over: 'Young Ron, come with me let's go to the wicket, what's your opinion?' As we walked out, I told him I knew nothing about wickets and said that it's the same whether we bat or bowl. All we have to do is bat and bowl better than them. Don seemed to accept that but I felt 10 feet tall and made 123 against Derek Shackleton while Tom got 104 and passed 40,000 career runs in the process. You had to play Shack late and in the V and with the full face; he could bowl so I rate this as one of my best innings.

The game took an interesting turn because while much of the play had been lost to bad weather on day two, Hampshire skipper Colin Ingleby-Mackenzie declared 146 runs behind during the third day lunch interval. Don promptly declared Worcestershire's second innings at 0 – 0 which left the home-side 147 to win in 159 minutes. Ron Headley said, 'I was frightened for the batsmen because over lunch the sun came out and as the first ball of the second innings was delivered it fetched a piece out and I was afraid that someone batting lower down like Shack would get hurt.'

Hampshire were dismissed for 31 in just 16 overs with Flavell claiming 5 – 9 and Coldwell 5 – 22. Michael Blair in the *Birmingham Post* described the events:

> The sun appeared from somewhere, hot and strong and blazing madly with a Worcestershire bias. It dried out the pitch with such ferocity that seasoned Worcestershire players admitted it was dangerous to bat on. Flavell, who had laboured for hours for nothing, suddenly found good-length deliveries jerking about like mortar shells. It was nine wins out of the last ten matches and a win in the next game at Sussex means they will complete one of the most extraordinary runs in their history. They are certainly playing well enough to deserve their luck. Kenyon would not expand on this other than to say, 'it is delicately poised.'

The reporter then made the telling comment that 'I fancy he smiled a bit when he said that.' It would appear Don was content that the destiny of the Championship was in his own hands. Ron Headley remarked, 'Towards the end of his career, Don would go through rough patches like this one but his value to the team was his leadership not his runs ... his quiet way of helping you get the best out of yourself is what made us Champions once more.'

Flavell, with 7 – 26, was again the destroyer as Sussex were bowled out for just 72, while Worcestershire replied with 166 giving them a lead of 94 runs on first innings. Sussex were dismissed for 225 (Gifford 5 – 71) second time around with Worcestershire set 132 to win in four hours and twenty minutes. On a pitch now behaving like the one at Bournemouth just a few days before, John Snow was proving a handful as he claimed 5 – 44. At 36 – 4 the tension mounted with

Filming the tense
finish at Hove in 1965
© Getty Images.

Don keeping cool enough to even film the last moments of the game as the visitors edged closer.

A priceless 38 from Booth, 31 not out from Richardson and 5 not out from Slade got Worcestershire over the line with 7 minutes of the season remaining. They had climbed to the top of the table for the first time in the season to pinch the Championship for the second successive year.

'Worcester Wobble In' was Patrick Robinson's headline in the *Daily Express* while the *Birmingham Post's* read: 'Last Lap of High Tension – but Courage Sees Them Through'.

The final words on the season belong to the captain who commented in the *Daily Express*: 'It has been a fantastic run; I would say that probably there has been nothing like it before.' Towards the end of the year the BBC broadcast a radio programme to mark the centenary of the formation of the club which included a series of interviews conducted by John Arlott who described Don as 'a superbly unruffled captain'. In it Don outlined the secret of success and in his own unique way, refers to his main strike bowler by his Christian name of John and not the nickname of Jack: 'We are a well-balanced side and with players in the John Flavell and Tom Graveney class, they did come off at a time when other players were sadly out of form. Coupling Tom and John together, from July through August, especially when the batsmen were out of form, they were instrumental in winning so many matches which clinched the Championship.' The essence of success is recorded in David Lemmon's *Official History of Worcestershire CCC* in which he states, 'Kenyon was in no doubt as to why the title was won: 'Complete team spirit and effort and a happy side.'

Don's return for the season though had been his worst since 1948. Just 458 runs at 14.31 with a highest score of 77 was out of character. In compensation, he had the satisfaction of knowing that he had led the County to a second successive Championship.

Celebrating the Championship at Hove, 1965. © Mirrorpix

Chapter 18

Jamaican Sun, Double Disappointment and Impending Retirement

A re-run of the previous season's lavish celebration dinner was held at the Indoor Bowling Club in Barneshall, Worcester on 16 November 1965. The bullish captain raised the stakes by stating that 'now we must aim for the treble' but in true form tempered this with a word of caution. Writing in his column in the *Sports Argus*, he commented, 'Personally I hope to be playing again next year but I must face that it could be my last season. We have to remember that I am no spring chicken and that there are several other members of our Championship side who are no longer in the flush of youth. Although we shall give other counties a good run for their money, we must always be on the lookout for new blood.'

Bob Carter, one of the unsung heroes of the side recalled,

> Don would work the seamers into the ground in an effort to win the game. He had the knack, however, of keeping you going. At six o'clock he would say 'take your time, you are on until seven' and do so with a caring arm around the shoulder. I remember when I was left out of the side, he would tell me in such a way that I could not get angry: 'I'll do you a favour today Bob, you can be twelfth man!' He was wise as captain, read pitches extremely well and his man management was second to none; there would be no public bollocking, just a quiet yet firm word – he was a stickler for discipline.

In March the team set out for a five match tour to Jamaica, organised by tobacco company, Carreras of Jamaica Ltd. Four, two-day matches plus a four day game were arranged. Each of the two day games were drawn, with Worcestershire passing 200 in each of their innings. In the four day game against a Jamaica Invitation XI at Montego Bay, Don contributed 45 and 25 with D'Oliveira hitting 101 in the second innings.

The home-side had put out their big guns, with Garry Sobers scoring 120 and Maurice Foster 73. Flavell returned the best figures (5 – 73) as the exercise proved its worth in providing some early season warm weather practice. With the new season about to start Don would again be absent at times on Test selector duty and yet more experiments to improve the game were introduced. Described as the 'height of idiocy' in his second volume of the *History of Worcestershire CCC,* W. R. Chignell stated, 'The decision was made to limit the first innings of each side to 65 overs in the first of the two matches between every two counties.' He concluded by saying that it was a 'resounding clanger because any batsman batting lower than number four was condemned to play utterly unnatural cricket.'

On the pitch, Garry Sobers was visiting with the touring West Indies side, but the early-May rain devastated the game with the home-side reaching 207 – 6. The *Birmingham Mail* painted a disturbing picture during the first game, with Michael Blair's headline *Post* reporting: 'Kenyon's Future in Balance'. He commented that 'it was almost a desperate search for form which drove Kenyon to the wicket, he should not have been playing; he knows that at forty-three he is batting for his cricketing future. His right ankle was damaged at the Warwickshire indoor nets two weeks ago and has not responded to treatment.

His all-important anchor foot will not support him as he goes across to the offside.' Somehow he muddled through and Worcestershire won the opener by six wickets against Glamorgan at Pontypridd. The *Evening Mail* commented, 'Captain Kenyon, showing a welcome return to top form dominated the partnership with Ormrod who defied a succession of Glamorgan bowling changes.' Don scored 46 in the second innings after Gifford had returned match figures of 10 – 67. Absent for the drawn game with Nottinghamshire, Don returned to score a second innings 64 against Sussex at New Road in another drawn game; the first of the sixty-five over experiment!

The first round of the Gillette Cup, now reduced to 60 overs a side, was successfully negotiated with a 19 run victory over Nottinghamshire at Worcester. Ron Headley with a 'painstaking and sensible' 64 was Man of the Match. The bookmakers immediately installed Worcestershire as 9/4 favourites for the competition, with neighbours Warwickshire quoted at 5/2.

When Kent visited New Road at the end of May, the news that everyone had been waiting for over the last twelve months arrived. The *Birmingham Post's* headline read: 'Kenyon 114 Sets Kent up for the Kill'. Michael Blair wrote,

> The New Road scoreboard, which has tended to blink rapidly past the symbol 'batsman No.1', got stuck there yesterday. Don Kenyon found his form with a bludgeoned 114.
>
> Thereafter the scoreboard went berserk. Kenyon had so knocked the stuffing out of Kent that, following the closure of Worcestershire's innings, in the next 90 minutes to the close, the visitors lost nine wickets for 73.

In scoring 37 in the second innings, Don passed 35,000 first class runs. Set 307 to win, Kent were dismissed for 226, to leave the home-side victors by 80 runs. The *Worcester News* also breathed a sigh of relief in reporting, 'Kenyon is still more than a shadowy figure of the past. In an aggressive three hours against Kent he reached the seventy-second century of his career, though it was his first since his 158 against Sussex at Eastbourne in August 1964.' A win at Romford against Essex by four wickets followed and then Northamptonshire were soundly beaten – in Don's absence – by 180 runs at Northampton. Brian Brain, standing in for Flavell who heard news of his father's death as the captains prepared to toss for innings, claimed 6 – 78 and 3 – 32 in a match-winning performance.

A 167 run thumping at the hands of Warwickshire was the first defeat of the

Boarding the plane for Jamaica in 1966. © EMPICSPA.

season with Tom Duckworth commenting in the *Sports Argus* that 'Worcestershire's batting, particularly the middle order, was looking frail and expressed his surprise that despite this, they were well placed in the table.' His other gripe was that the fielding was poor and that 'the task of hiding several elderly players unable to move around quickly is taxing even Don Kenyon's resources.'

Never regarded as one of the best fielders, Don was showing the signs of slowing down too. In my meeting with John Elliott, he recalled, 'Roy Booth refers to Don as 'steel fingers' he was not one of the best fielders, especially as he got older.' A full strength batting line up was 'put out' for the nine wicket win over Cambridge University, with Don (49) Ormrod (42) and Horton (91) making best use of the practice time. In his next eight innings, Don only mustered 91 runs with a top score of just 26 in Roy Booth's benefit game against Yorkshire. Roy recalls how Don typically would raise his game against Yorkshire. It was not unusual for there to be some spark or other, and have noted previously about a run-in Don had with Fred Trueman. Roy recounted, 'I remember one occasion, the Yorkshire fielders were chirping away so Don stopped the game and as he walked a few paces away from the crease he commented, "When you've finished your chat I'll come in and bat again." It had the desired effect and they quietened down. You didn't mess with Don.'

These Championship matches were punctuated with an 82 run win over Essex in the second round of the Gillette Cup with Horton (51) and Ormrod (50) setting up the victory. A second hundred of the season followed in a fourth straight draw, this time against Northamptonshire at Worcester in early July. 'A Masterly Knock from Kenyon' was the headline in the *Birmingham Post,* which commented, 'Kenyon made 103 out of the first 176 in a shade under four hours. He remains one of the readiest murderers of the ball in England and as the Northamptonshire attack was scarcely better than willing he took his toll. He hit 11 fours in his innings and provided the substance while Headley (72 not out) provided the glitter.' On five occasions out of the last six games, Worcestershire had failed to bowl out the opposition on the last day; it meant that Yorkshire had opened up a forty-two point lead at the top of the table. The *Birmingham Post* suggested that 'the champion instinct, therefore, has faded.'

Better was to follow with a four wicket victory over Leicestershire at Leicester with Don hitting 57 in the first innings and D'Oliveira claiming 5 – 49 in Leicestershire's second innings to help set up the victory. The *Sunday Telegraph* described Don's innings as 'elegant' and went on to say, 'Kenyon batted as befits a Test selector. He hooked five imperious boundaries and stroked Lock for an effortless straight six before he dragged a ball from Marner onto his stumps.' Missing the draw against Gloucestershire due to Test duties, Don returned to captain Worcestershire to a ten wicket victory in the return fixture where the two sides played each other for six out of seven straight days.

In the *Sports Argus* on 16 July, Don described his 'royal week' where he and Jean had been invited to the Queen's Garden Party at Buckingham Palace. Don said he had 'had quite a chat' with the Duke of Edinburgh who is well versed in the game.' As if one visit was not enough, Don and Jean were to attend a second Garden Party in 1992.

In the next six games, two were lost (to Kent and Leicestershire), one was drawn and three wins secured. The first of the victories came against Surrey by an innings and 14 runs. Flavell with 7 – 58 and 4 – 38 was the destroyer while Don contributed a useful 40 out of a total of 269. A three wicket victory at Edgbaston followed, with Don striking 56 in the first innings. Worcestershire were indebted to 94 from Graveney and 70 from D'Oliveira in the second innings in pursuit of the 247 victory target, which was achieved off the fifth ball of the last over.

The next victory came in another thriller against Derbyshire at Ilkeston. With Graveney and D'Oliveira playing for England at Headingley, Don dropped himself to number three to allow Duncan Fearnley to open with Horton. In reply to Worcestershire's 210 (Kenyon 34), Derbyshire could only muster 180 but the home-side struck back as Worcestershire were dismissed for just 107 in their second 'dig.' Bowling through several showers, Gifford came to the rescue to claim 8 – 54 from 34 overs, to help clinch victory by just three runs. The concern during the game was that Don had to leave the field with a leg muscle injury; this made him a doubt for the Gillette Cup semi-final tie with Hampshire.

The following day, there was no improvement in Don's condition, so Graveney took over the captaincy. In front of a big New Road crowd, Hampshire opted to field first and ran into the 'in form' Martin Horton who, with the help of D'Oliveira (44) smashed 114 out of a total of 253 – 4. Hampshire were always behind the rate and with Coldwell claiming 4 – 39 plus Flavell and Carter picking up two wickets apiece, Worcestershire booked their place in the final by a 99 run margin, Horton was deservedly named Man of the Match.

Three days later, once more in the absence of the captain, Worcestershire wrapped up a seven wicket victory over Derbyshire at Kidderminster thanks to 112 from Fearnley, the replacement opener for Kenyon, who struck his maiden first-class century. With Gifford (6 – 55) and Horton (4 – 85) in great form, Derbyshire's second innings was restricted to 188. The home-side knocked off the 134 for victory in just under two hours.

The title race was hotting up, because as Worcestershire won, leaders Yorkshire suffered a defeat at the hands of Surrey which meant that their lead at the top was now just eighteen points. Kenyon's title race stuttered when he returned for the clash against Somerset at New Road, with the visitors winning by 127 runs. Revenge was taken in the return fixture later in the same week when Gifford and Horton shared thirteen wickets in an eight wicket victory. Don stayed at number three while Fearnley continued to justify his spot as opener with more assured knocks of 37 and 32 across both games.

The race to the title got even closer in the next round of matches with Worcestershire hammering Middlesex at Lord's in two days to win by an innings and 41 runs. In reply to Middlesex's 115, the visitors' 219 was enough to ensure victory with Don (back to opener) scoring 33 and Graveney propping up the innings with 72. Flavell with 5 – 28 and D'Oliveira 5 – 14 took just 65 minutes to inflict the heavy defeat.

The *Daily Mirror* captured the moment with the headline: 'The Kenyon Killers do it Again' as Worcestershire closed the gap on Yorkshire to just six points as the Tykes were defeated by Warwickshire at The Circle in Hull. With just two matches left, Worcestershire were derailed by the weather. Over the three day period only the equivalent of a full day's play was possible yet in that time Worcestershire had the upper hand over Essex at Worcester. Graveney (166) and D'Oliveira (126) enabled Don to declare at 405 – 6. With Essex languishing on 122 – 7 (Flavell 5 – 51) in reply, the weather intervened to thwart the progress of Kenyon's men. Yorkshire fared little better and picked up no points in the drawn game with Surrey at The Oval. The equation was simple. In the final match of the Championship season Worcestershire needed to beat Sussex and were relying on Kent to either draw with or beat Yorkshire to prevent them from winning the title.

At the close of day two, Michael Blair's headline in the *Birmingham Post* painted a bleak but accurate picture: 'Severe Setback to Hat-Trick Hopes'. His report stated, 'The New Road pitch behaved badly, Worcestershire fielded badly and batted even worse. They dropped their catches as Sussex made 145, which looked a formidable total as the home-side lost four wickets for 8 runs and it needed a grim fight from the tail to take the total to 77, their lowest of the season.'

In spite of Flavell leading the fight back in the second innings with 7 – 36 to dismiss the visitors for just 115, Worcestershire fell short of their victory target of 182 and were dismissed for 150. The 'local Worcestershire lad' from

Peopleton, Sussex's John Snow (9 – 88) and Tony Buss (9 – 86) did the damage for the visitors.

It was all academic, as Yorkshire beat Kent at Harrogate by the slim margin of 24 runs to be crowned champions. The consolation for Kenyon's team was the runners up spot, they still had chance to redeem themselves in the Gillette Cup Final on the following day. Even as the preparations were being made, Tom Duckworth in the *Sports Argus* had already begun the enquiry into the disappointing end to the season. 'Worcestershire Home Form was the Downfall' was the headline, Duckworth continued, 'Of their twelve county games played at New Road they won only three, drew five and lost four. Of the other two games, one was won at Kidderminster and the other at Dudley was a draw.'

He went on to pinpoint some other critical factors, 'Skipper Don Kenyon who again led the side with great skill and shrewdness had a much better season. But with many players in the veteran of near veteran stage Worcestershire must be looking anxiously at their reserve strength. In a few years' time a good many replacements will be needed and whether they have sufficient young players of quality to take over from the men who have served them so well has still to be proved.' Attention could now switch to the Final at Lord's. Billed in the *Birmingham Post and Mail's* sports supplement as: 'Day of Decision for the Midland Rivals', the game appeared to be an evenly balanced contest.

Brian Brain was included at the expense of Ron Headley and with Don winning the toss, he elected to bat. With the score on 33 Don hit wicket, bowled Rudi Webster for 13. I spoke with M. J. K. Smith, the victorious Warwickshire captain, who had vivid memories of the Final: 'Rudi Webster was from the West Indies and was much underrated. He got his wickets at less than twenty apiece which is one hell of a record, he was useful. He'd been a medical student up in Edinburgh and we took him on; good bowler.'

Worcestershire managed to get to 155 – 8 off their 60 overs, but Warwickshire got home comfortably by five wickets thanks to 66 from Man of the Match Bob Barber. M. J. K. Smith told me:

Don had a great career which demonstrated what a great player he was. Technically very orthodox he suffered immediately after the war with lack of opportunity. I got on well with him and enjoyed his company, he was a smashing chap.

There were many high-class players but the bottom line is nobody will query his cricketing ability. As a captain, although I never played under him, he had a damn good side especially with Flavell and Coldwell in it. Good captains have good sides and Worcestershire were and this reflected in Don's leadership qualities.

In '66, Tommy Cartwright took 3 – 16 from his 12 overs. Like Derek Shackleton they bowled at mine and your pace but were the most successful bowlers in the country. They were a nuisance if you played against them because with Tommy in particular, five out of six balls would hit the stumps. I remember him 'doing' Tom (Graveney) to a great catch from Billy Ibadulla at short leg. We would look after Tommy because he was so vital to the attack and then Billy would nip in when the crash was on and take vital wickets (2 – 33 from 9 overs in the Final)

Bob Barber won the Man of the Match. He changed his religion from a nudger and nurdler when he came to us. Things hadn't worked out for him at Lancashire and when he left he started putting bat to ball. His change of attitude came about due to the change in the no ball law. Originally it had been the back foot rule and with drag, bowlers would rough up outside off stump on a decent length. When the front foot law came in it cut that out and he could play with more freedom.

I was a little surprised that Worcestershire did not want us to have first use of the pitch so I was not disappointed when Don decided to bat. As we know, bowling first in September at Lord's can be an advantage.

The *Sunday Express'* headline on 4 September did not make for happy reading when it stated, 'Two black days and Worcester lose the lot'. Denis Compton summed up the end of the season: 'To a fighting bunch of cricketers like Don Kenyon's men there is nothing like consolation in being double runners up. Yesterday though they ran out of steam as their batting depressingly fell apart in the face of an accurate Warwickshire attack.'

Personally, Don had improved on 1965 with 1,091 runs at 27.27 which included two centuries and three half-centuries. With an eye on the future, Geoffrey Beane in the *Birmingham Post* reported, 'Kenyon to Sign New Contract'. In it Don stated, 'The club have offered me another year's contact and as far as it is possible to plan ahead I hope to be playing in championship cricket again in 1967. I have certain business commitments which are important to me, but my employers have again kindly agreed to let me play on if I wish to.'

Don was in bullish mood at the start of the 1967 season, writing his column for the *Sports Argus*, on Saturday 22 April he stated, 'We want the double! – why not, the ability is here.' He continued, 'We have been practicing hard for a fortnight and have arranged a couple of one-day warm up games against Gloucestershire at New Road.' He also paid tribute to Martin Horton who had taken up a coaching appointment in New Zealand and commented that without Gilbert Parkhouse as coach (he had taken a post as sports master

With M. J. K. Smith after the Gillette Cup Final in 1966. © EMPICSPA.

at Melville College, Edinburgh), the onus would be on the senior players to bridge that gap.

A week after these words were penned, Worcestershire were dumped out of the Gillette Cup at the first hurdle, a two wicket defeat at the hands of Sussex at New Road. Needing 116 to win, Sussex reached 89 – 6 but recovered sufficiently to edge home. Sussex' Mike Buss with 4 – 25 was named as Man of the Match.

The opening first-class fixture against the Indians was ruined by rain but not before Basil D'Oliveira had thumped a belligerent 174 not out as Worcestershire declared on 335 – 6. In reply, India could only muster 106 – 8 with Len Coldwell the pick of the bowlers claiming 4 – 39. Don's observations of the D'Oliveira innings summed up his approach to batting: 'When Basil hits the ball with the middle of the bat it stays hit. He batted as well as we have seen him since joining the staff, a most encouraging sight for us.'

A draw in the opening Championship game against Lancashire at Old Trafford was followed by a five-wicket defeat at the hands of Yorkshire played at Hull. The Lancashire game was ground breaking in that play on day two was scheduled for a Sunday, further evidence that the game was beginning to move into a new era. Don commented that his only objection to this was that play could not start until two o' clock, which made for a short day, but this was compensated for by a longer day on the Monday. It also meant that some players would lose out on the income from benefit fixtures, traditionally held on a Sunday.

The defeat at Hull drew an honest assessment from Don who also expressed his displeasure at the pitch. Speaking to Jack Godfrey in the *Worcester Evening News* he commented, 'We won the toss and we should have won the match, but the plain truth is that we are playing badly at the moment. The pitch must also be classed as unsuitable for first-class cricket, it exploded from the word go.'

A ten-wicket victory in a low scoring game against Somerset at Worcester gave the County its first victory of the season. Jack Flavell with match figures of 9 – 68 and Len Coldwell with 9 – 109 destroyed the visitors for 80 and 112. Roy Booth celebrated his 1,000th victim during the game when he caught his opposite number Geoff Clayton off Coldwell for 19 in the second innings.

Two further drawn games against Essex and Leicestershire followed, it was now the end of May and Don had still to reach his first 50 of the season. The 'curse of the drawn game' was also to follow Worcestershire throughout 1967, they finished drawing sixteen in total yet finished a creditable fifth position in the Championship. Don's indifferent run continued in the innings and two run defeat against Yorkshire at Kidderminster where he was dismissed for 19 and 29. He was criticised too for electing to bat rather than inviting the visitors to have first use of the pitch. He quantified this in the *Sports Argus* by stating, 'On reflection I would have done the same thing again in similar circumstances. And while it was an easy decision to take, Brian Close, the Yorkshire and England skipper, told me that he would have done exactly the same had he won the toss.'

Three consecutive draws followed against Warwickshire, Derbyshire and Middlesex, the outstanding performances during that time being Headley (104) and Graveney (113 not out) versus Warwickshire, while Norman Gifford claimed 7 – 72 in the same fixture. At Derby, Don recorded his first half-century of the season (72) with Michael Blair in the *Birmingham Post* stating that 'Kenyon

Plays his Luck.' He wrote, 'Don Kenyon, like a skipper who had forgotten the plan, walked through a minefield at Derby yesterday and miraculously escaped the explosions Harold Rhodes (4 – 22) caused all around him and emerged with 72 runs which could well settle the match.'

56 from Don was the only consolation from the innings and 117 run defeat against Surrey at the Oval in mid-June, Ken Barrington with a first innings 142 not out and Pat Pocock with match figures of 11 – 115 doing the damage for the home-side. Away on Test selector duty for the 202 run defeat against Kent at Tunbridge Wells, Don's next three innings yielded just 45 runs, but in the second innings against Middlesex at Worcester in late June, a 74 brought a glimmer of hope of better things to come. The report in the *Worcester News* stated, 'Don Kenyon, timing and directing his shots splendidly, today made his best score of the season, in two and a quarter hours, to help a more resolute Worcestershire establish a promising position against Middlesex.' Despite this effort, the visitors, knocked off the 286 required for victory for the loss of six wickets thanks to 162 not out from Peter Parfitt.

The defeat left Worcestershire languishing in fifteenth place in the table and over the weekend of 30 June and 1 July, the news broke of Don's decision to retire at the end of the season. The reasons behind his decision along with detail of his last century, scored just five days after the announcement, are documented in my opening chapter, but there was still the remainder of the season to be played. Prior to Don's last appearance at New Road, he featured in eight Championship games of which three were won and five were drawn. Away on Test selector duties he missed the two further drawn games against Glamorgan and Nottinghamshire respectively. His best score in that time was 96 in the second innings of the match against Derbyshire at New Road, but his tally of 316 was a disappointing return.

One could argue that the balance of power was shifting further from Don towards some of the younger players. During this eight match period Duncan Fearnley, Ted Hemsley and Alan Ormrod hit two half-centuries apiece while the responsibility to score consistently rested with Ron Headley, Tom Graveney and Basil D'Oliveira who all hit centuries.

The transition of power in the batting line up was completed during Don's last appearance at New Road against the touring Pakistan side in the third week of August, when Glenn Turner made his first-class debut for the County. The story of Don's last appearance at New Road and Glenn's first also feature in chapter one. Turner was to become the mainstay of the Worcestershire battling line up for the next fourteen seasons, he wore Kenyon's crown well.

In his penultimate game Don scored 22 and 9 in the innings and 48 run defeat against Leicestershire at Leicester, but he signed off with a second innings 67 not out at Colwyn Bay in the draw against Glamorgan. His final knock was described in the Club's 1968 Yearbook as a 'typically masterly innings lasting 77 minutes'. True to him 'being his own man' he had signed off his career in typical style by passing 37,000 first-class runs in the process.

His final tally of 34,490 first-class runs for Worcestershire remains a club record and even eclipses Graeme Hick's phenomenal career tally of 31,149. This statistic alone underscores Don's ability as a top class batsman.

The end of the season also brought the retirement of two more of the greats, Jack Flavell and Dick Richardson, both of whom had served the County with huge distinction; their records also speak volumes.

Flavell's final delivery claimed the wicket of Brian Statham; in an eighteen year career he claimed 1,507 first-class wickets which puts him third in the all-time list for Worcestershire bowlers behind Norman Gifford and Reg Perks. Richardson scored 15,843 runs between 1952 and 1967 which places him in thirteenth place in Worcestershire's all-time records.

News of the new captain was made public with Alex Bannister writing in the *Daily Mail*, 31 October: 'Graveney Takes over Captaincy from Kenyon.' Tom commented, 'It will be hard to follow "Dono" although he never cracked the whip he had authority and was highly successful in results and with the team.' Praise indeed from one of the greats of the game.

Chapter 19

Boycott Dropped, the D'Oliveira Affair, Club Presidency and a Brush with Royalty

When Don's career began to dim in 1967, he was still one of the Test selectors and was involved in controversy as early as June. During the Leeds Test, Geoffrey Boycott was dropped after scoring 246 not out against India. He batted six hours on day one to close on 106 not out. John Woodcock from *The Times* said, 'He had set out to be there at the close regardless of his responsibilities as a public entertainer.' Boycott did score quicker on the second day, outstripping D'Oliveira, but it was not enough to save him. He was dropped, not for slow scoring, but 'as a disciplinary measure.'

In the summer of 2014 I spoke to Geoffrey about his recollections of this in conjunction with his opinions on Don. He told me:

Worcestershire beat us at Worcester in 1964, I was only a young kid then; Flavell and Coldwell did the damage we were well beaten. Worcester was always fast then, quick and bouncy unlike Headingley. When we played there, we were caught out because there was no other surface like it to play on. I didn't play much against Worcester once I got in the England side – I'd miss ten games a season.

Flavell got me first innings, I never did well against him, and Coldwell in the second. (lbw Flavell 0 and bowled Coldwell 7). I recall Don getting a ton, (113) he made his runs easily it was so bloody quick. He looked a good player but this was probably the only time I played against him at Worcester. [Geoffrey was correct, Jack Flavell dismissed him for 11 at New Road in 1965 when Don was away on Test selection duty and the only other time he played against Don in Worcestershire was at Kidderminster in 1967.]

We went to Lord's for a trial game and Ray Illingworth said it was the best thing getting out cheaply. He told me I was in good nick (I had just got three hundreds) and that I had got out to two very good bowlers and that in doing so it would sharpen my game; he was right.

I asked Geoffrey what was said to him when he was dropped from the Test team and how the decision had been explained to him, he said:

Nobody spoke to me; it was terrible their man management left a lot to be desired. When they dropped me, yes Don was a selector, but as such a young guy I wanted someone to explain to me what happened; nobody asked me any questions it was an amazing situation.

All I can say is that when I subsequently met Don, he seemed a decent fellow and was a good bat. He was not in his pomp when I played against him, but his record stands up.

In typical Boycott style he closed by saying, 'At least I phoned you up lad, but that's all I can really remember.'

Martin Jackson, Don's son-in-law, recalls answering a call from Geoffrey, one Sunday lunchtime, wanting to speak to Don at the time of his dropping from the side. I enquired as to what happened, but as Martin said, 'Don in true form did not comment at all. We knew Boycott had been on the phone, but he would never talk about his cricket in this way.'

At the same time as the Boycott incident, Don received a letter from MCC Secretary, Colonel S. C. 'Billy' Griffith inviting him to sit on the selection panel for the upcoming winter tour to the West Indies. I stumbled across this when reviewing the outstanding MCC archive early in 2015. While the responses to the invitation from Don's contemporaries are formal, his is quite the opposite and captures a sense of playfulness which does not conform to the perception of 'dour Don' to which Duncan Fearnley sometimes refers. In his own hand he writes: 'Dear Col – delighted to accept the invitation to serve on the selection committee for 67/68 tour. P.s. would be available to go myself if there's a spare ticket etc.! (Manager, scorer, follower ...)'

In March 1968, Don's career was commemorated with the planting of a Copper Beech tree at New Road. In the floods of 2008 it succumbed to the impact of the summer floods and had to be felled, a sad moment to lose this strong link with the past.

As 1968 was to progress, little did we know that Don would have a critical part to play in one of cricket's most notorious events; the D'Oliveira affair.

The selection meeting at Lord's to choose the MCC team to tour South Africa in 1968/69 was scheduled for 8.00 p.m. on 27 August. Speculation had been rife for some time whether Basil D'Oliveira would be included or not, especially as there were rumblings from South Africa that he would not be welcome on account of the Apartheid regime.

D'Oliveira, who had not had a good tour to the West Indies during the previous winter, had to prove he was worthy of inclusion; his 158 in the Oval Test against Australia went some way to helping his cause. Eight people convened at 8.00 p.m. to select the party and did not adjourn until 1.50 a.m. the following day.

Although senior figures from the MCC were present, Don was one of the four selectors, his role was described by Peter Oborne in *Basil D'Oliveira – Cricket and Conspiracy the Untold Story*:

Of all the people in the room Kenyon was the most remote from the establishment. He had a special role on the committee. The other selectors, thanks to their business commitments, could watch only the occasional match.

As captain of Worcestershire, Kenyon saw the game at first hand every day and was able to bring bulletins from the county game. Only a player like Kenyon, who was ready to accept that his own prospects of playing Test cricket had gone, could fulfil this invaluable role.

Right: Planting the Copper
Beech Tree, March 1968. ©
Berrows Newspapers.

Below: Lord's selection meeting.
© Getty Images

D'Oliveira was not selected, but nearly three weeks later Tom Cartwright was declared unfit and D'Oliveira was included in the squad as his replacement.

The minutes of a follow up the meeting at 4.00 p.m. on Monday 16 September state, 'Cartwright replaced, D'Oliveira comes in, Jones is fit, [reference to Jeff Jones who had to prove his fitness over two days' practice] no wives before Christmas and any stay limited to six weeks maximum.' In Basil D'Oliveira's *The D'Oliveira Affair*, he recounts the response from the South African Prime Minister: 'It's not the MCC team, it's the team of the Anti-Apartheid Movement. We are not prepared to accept a team thrust upon us ... it is the team of political opponents of South Africa. It is a team of people who don't care about sports relations at all.' S. C. Griffith the Secretary of MCC responded, 'Our position is clear. If the chosen team is not acceptable to South Africa, the MCC will call off the tour.' And so it was!

It has been widely reported that Don was an advocate of D'Oliveira's and had always promoted his Worcestershire colleague to be chosen to represent England. Mike Vockins kindly spoke on my behalf to the then Chairman of selectors, Doug Insole, and asked him of his recollections:

> Don took over from Willie Watson and was good news. At that point we always wanted a current player, but even if Don hadn't been a player though, we would still have wanted him. He was a sound judge of a player and sound with his opinions. He was well respected by other captains and when he went round the grounds he'd ask the opposition captain for his views; he always spoke to the umpires as well. The measure of how we rated him was that we still wanted him after he finished playing. Don was very straight at the time of the Basil issue; he was pro Basil and played a big part in the discussion.
>
> The tour to South Africa was to be led by Colin Cowdrey with Les Ames as manager, but following Basil's disappointing tour to the West Indies the previous winter the selectors had their doubts. When Bas got his hundred at The Oval though, it made it hard not to pick him; however, from the perspective of those in the room his omission was entirely a cricketing decision.

Away from Test selection duties, Don was still working for the Dudley Iron and Steel Company. He found time to enjoy a round of golf or some time on the practice range at Enville Golf Club, especially on his way home from work. Jean Kenyon recalls how Don would get up early and be out of the house for eight o'clock on a Sunday morning so that he could get in a round of golf before lunch.

In April 1971, Don and Jean attended a reception at Downing Street to commemorate England's winning of The Ashes in Australia during the winter. Don maintained the opportunity to be involved in cricket as a Man of the Match adjudicator for the Gillette Cup knockout matches from 1968 until 1972 and was elected as the first President of Stourbridge Cricket Society, a post he held from its inception in 1972 until his death in 1996. Don also served on the Worcestershire General Committee from 1968; however, in 1976 things were to change when he was appointed to the Cricket Sub-Committee following a turbulent winter for the club.

The Worcestershire Club Yearbook in its review of 1976 referred to the closing months of 1975 as a 'winter of discontent.' It continued,

> There were a number of issues that became interwoven and confused but the major issue, and the one which caused the most controversy and debate, was the committee's decision to retain, for 1976, a much reduced playing staff based on three reasons:
> It had become apparent that the staff, as then structured, was unlikely to repeat its previous successes.
> Financial reasons.
> The need to give the talented younger players more first team opportunities.

Club Secretary at the time, Mike Vockins explained to me the detail behind the incident:

> I told everyone that it would be better if the club called a meeting to explain its policy, therefore, it was arranged and scheduled to be held in the Shirehall. The queue of people was across the Shirehall car park and extended around the corner. We had put up a sound system in another room but because people said they could not see or hear we had to postpone the meeting.
> We reconvened the special meeting at The Malvern Winter Gardens. The chairman of the Cricket Sub-Committee was Dick Howorth, a very genuine chap, who unfortunately was asked a loaded question which had significant consequences for him. He was not a public speaker and fluffed his lines which gave the impression he did not know what he was on about. It came to a vote, he was not re-elected and never came to the ground again; it broke his heart.
> There was a change in committee, one particular one being that Don was appointed chairman of the Cricket Sub-Committee in succession to Dick Howorth. We had a committee of fifty-four which was very unwieldy and made it hard to make decisions; it was later trimmed down.

By 1980 Don had been made Vice-Pesident of the club and in 1982 Mike Jones succeeded him as Chairman of the Cricket Sub-Committee. The club had not yet finished with the man who captained them to dual County Championships, and higher office was shortly to be bestowed upon him. In 1986 Duncan Fearnley was elected as Chairman and was firmly in favour of Don succeeding the Duke of Westminster as President. Mike Vockins commented,

> We raised the idea at a meeting which was warmly welcomed, he proved to be a brilliant President. He served for three years and was at the ground a lot and supported the players. He was sensible towards them because he didn't talk 'in my day', he was good news.
> We were lucky because, in George Chesterton who followed Don, we had experienced a golden period of three great and immensely popular presidents. Don did everything asked of him and set the tone well. It didn't matter who came to the club, whether or not he was hosting well-known personalities to lunch, everyone liked him and he did it so well; he was so good for the committee.

With the dynamic Duncan Fearnley as Chairman and the hugely respected Don Kenyon as President, the last piece of the jigsaw was the maturing of the Club's most successful Captain, Phil Neale. It's always a delight to talk to Phil, so when I caught up with him during 2014, I asked him to recall his memories of Don:

> If I ever join the committee I'd like to think I'd remember what it was like to be a player because D. K. was never one to throw the past at me. He accepted the fact that things were different and he'd sit in committee meetings and back me 100 per cent. I enjoyed having him there he was always prepared to see my point of view and support it. He would place total faith in me, and while we debated the issues, he always believed the captain should get what he wants.
>
> I liked to talk to players from previous generations, like Roly Jenkins, they might tell the same story but there's always good stuff in it; I listened, learned and took out the things which I felt no longer applied. I have to think hard today because of influences like law/rule changes. It's a nightmare for a captain now because he is always a fielder short due to fielding restrictions. Alongside the range of shots the players play, you can only limit the damage done. One has to make allowances how the game changes, I firmly believe that D. K. would have done that. Always a good guy to talk to I didn't spend as much time with him as I should have. He was never one to push forward or keep coming into the dressing room, although he was welcome. He spoke more in the committee room when we had a drink.
>
> Don was from a totally different environment but didn't force it on to me. The key thing is the principles, the basics which don't change, for example, how you manage players and get the best out of bowlers.
>
> Looking at the statistics for that side in the 1960s, there were a lot of good players but that doesn't make a good team. There would be big egos and someone had to get the best out of them. I hear stories of Flav and Coldwell going to the nets, bowling two bouncers and coming out again, but if people deliver, they can do that. Like Botham – the key is that he delivered!
>
> His help was needed most as president and during cricket committee meetings. I remember fondly as a former county captain him being there for me; if I needed support, I had it and valued it. I'd come away from meetings and say to Chris [Phil's wife] that 'I'm glad Don Kenyon was there tonight just to give me the bit of support I needed.'
>
> If you have played in a previous era you have to spend time to see and understand the problems the modern player faces. Until you understand it, don't tell them how to play the modern game, Don had the knack of getting it just right.

Phil refers in passing to Ian Botham who had joined the club in 1987. When it was known that there was a possibility of him coming to New Road, there were many rumours circulating as to how this would be viewed. One was that Don would resign from the club over it; however, Mike Vockins recounts the true version of events:

> Phil instigated the move. He picked up that Beefy was unhappy at Somerset, not just over them sacking Richards and Garner. In committee we had one of the best ever debates. Duncan was not the most natural chair, he tended to let things drift

in the formalities of conducting a meeting, but on that occasion he said everyone must speak. I'll hold my hands up, I was wrong to doubt the signing. I thought we had such a good young team, someone from another county might be a bit jaundiced and not help the young players; I was wrong.

As I recall, Don was very positive and said that that we should go ahead and sign him. He got on well with Beefy, if you asked him he would speak of Don in a respectful voice; they spoke as equals, giants in their own context.

Worcestershire won the County Championship in 1988, retained it in 1989 and were presented with the Lord's Taverners' Trophy by HRH The Duke of Edinburgh at Buckingham Palace.

In the winter of 1989/90, the cricket suite at New Road was established to provide improved dining and catering facilities all year round. Two rooms were dedicated to Reg Perks and The Foster family, while Don's contribution to Worcestershire cricket was recognised with the main function room being named after him, the Don Kenyon Room.

In July 1992, Don and Jean were invited to attend the Garden Party at Buckingham Palace in aid of the Central Council of Physical Recreation. The invitation refers to achieving 'world championship status', recognition for the side who took cricket to the world in 1965 and achieved so much.

Throughout the late 1980s and into the early nineties, Don continued to visit New Road and kept a watching brief over his grandson Daniel who was born during the first game of the 1987 season. During that time he took great delight in attending the annual old players reunion.

Don as President with Worcestershire captain Phil Neale, celebrating the Championship title in 1988. © Berrows Newspapers.

Chapter 20

A Family Affair, the Doting Grandfather, World Tour Re-Visited and the Kenyon Award

Putting the family first was paramount in everything Don did; the wellbeing and security of his wife and daughters came first. It's only fitting that Jean, their daughters Lesley Kenyon, Sue Jackson and her husband Martin plus their son Daniel draw his story to a close.

Sue

The cricketers were his second family, but not being outgoing he found it hard and never liked being away from home. He was incredibly shy as a youngster, which could have been taken as off-hand. He was similar in character to Dan, who also doesn't like meeting new people.

Dan

We used to go to the cricket a lot, he taught me to enjoy it and not to be serious especially at a young age. Wearing his Worcester sweater, he used to throw balls to me on the outfield but he would never coach me. Nan would always traipse behind us, out of the limelight, she preferred that. He took me everywhere, for instance to signings or cricket society meetings, it's just a shame he never saw me play. He wasn't pushy and wouldn't impose himself. He let me get on with how I wanted to approach any situation.

Playing in the nets once, someone stood behind us and told him that he ought to teach me to play the defensive shot. He said 'no, I want him to enjoy it and just play.' He didn't coach but would pass on information if he was asked. He was physically very strong and like him I have strong arms and neck. I am like him in other ways too, especially in personality and character.

I enjoy my own company and do not find meeting new people easy, he was like that too. Nan tells me when he was dropping her off at a friend's house once, he was asked if he wanted to go in and simply replied, 'Not really.' He didn't equate with idle talk and as it was not one of his friends it didn't bother him whether he met them or not. Just like me, he didn't like meeting new people or to talk just for the sake of it.

Yet if we had to walk from one side of the ground to the other it would take hours, he'd always give people time, he loved being there. As we drove in, he'd talk to the gate men then we'd wander over to the playground area by the old scoreboard and sometimes play there with Basil's grandchildren, Brett and Marcus.

Lesley

Like Dad I'll contribute if it adds value but I won't just talk for the sake of it. He could be a bit abrupt sometimes and it could come across like that but he did what he wanted. I wouldn't think of him either as having a real sense of humour. In general he was a serious man; whatever he did his approach was to be professional, even once he had retired.

He never got angry with us as children, never raised his voice but took life as it came. If anyone ever asked him about us, he'd simply say, 'Talk to their mother, she has brought them up.'

Dan

He was always relaxed as a grandparent, never raised his voice and was softly spoken. I used to go and stay with him and Nan one day a week until I started school. He'd always make bacon and egg for breakfast then he would go to the greenhouse for hours on end. He would fill – all that I could describe as shallow oven trays – full of water for the birds and I'd tip them out just to tease him, but he didn't lose his temper.

I remember holidays. I used to go to Swanage with him and Nan each year. He was mesmerised by arcades, we'd go in twice a day where he won loads of soft toys. He had brilliant eye hand co-ordination to operate the grabber. He was a creature of habit and would, like me, go to the same restaurant and eat the same thing each time. He was a man of routine, so with cricket being a game of so many routines he would feel comfortable.

I think Nan and Grandad were going to move to Swanage but when I was born it changed everything, and they decided to stay in Stourbridge. The draw of family was too much for him to move then, which typifies him precisely.

Sue

Until about the age of twelve we didn't have holidays with Dad. Mom, Lesley and I would pack our stuff into a Mini Traveller and off we'd go to the caravan in Tal-y-Bont. The first holiday abroad was a cruise. This was our first big collective holiday, and we had new frocks for dinner and evenings. After driving to Southampton we embarked on the ship and mom immediately went to bed and was sick for five days. We went through a force eight gale in the Bay of Biscay which wasn't pleasant. Dad and I were fine but even in the pool there was a swell because of the weather. As I got out of the lift one day I put my foot in a pool of sick. I marched to our cabin, and said 'you'll never guess what some dirty person did?' … My sister confessed to it being her!

The doting grandfather, with grandson Daniel. From the Kenyon family collection.

Lesley

I remember the cruise holiday, we stopped off at Madeira, The Canaries, Casablanca and Tangiers. Yes, The Bay of Biscay was very rough but Dad was a very good sailor. While mom was ill, he would spend all of his time on deck, even in the rough conditions he could be found on deck and made sure he had his three meals a day. He was very much a creature of habit, for instance, before he went to bed he would put everything out on the dressing table ready for the next morning.

We had two weeks away at the end of each season, once he was away from cricket he was in a different world. I had a place in Swanage at one point, when I worked in London, mom, Dad and Dan would sometimes come and stay, they loved it, he was very content when he was down there.

Martin

He had his life mapped out with his family. I remember in Majorca once, a car pulled up and the bloke recognised Don, but he didn't go out of his way to be well known, he was more concerned about us and Jean.

Sue

Dad taught me to catch a cricket ball so I could play rounders, but other than that he was not a player of games until Dan came along. We never did things like playing cricket on the beach; I think he wanted a break from it.

We then talked some more about cricketing recollections.

Sue

He liked India but didn't like the way the rich treated the poor. He said the crowds were amazing and he liked playing there. He enjoyed the heat and being outside in it. At home first thing in a morning he'd open the back door and be outside, from morning to night, even in winter he'd be out there with just his coat on.

In India they stayed in maharajahs' palaces, where if you dropped a shirt it was taken, washed and returned in the blink of an eye. If you stepped outside, though, the poverty was unbearable, he didn't like that. I know that he was awe struck by the Taj Mahal, it had a real impact on him, especially its splendour.

Mom tells the story [that] he was at a dinner in London during a game against India when someone identified him as a cricketer but thought he was Indian because he was so dark skinned. They even asked him how he was settling in, much to his amusement.

Jean

During the 1951/52 tour, the players attended a dinner hosted by the Maharajah of Visianagaram, known simply as Vizzy. Each of the players were given a black evening clutch bag to take home as a gift to their loved one. A peacock, embroidered in silk is on the front, beautifully decorated too with green and turquoise bead work. On the back it says, 'MCC from Vizzy'. A lovely thing, I still have mine.

He would write virtually every day, the letters were frequent. He always numbered them, so that if one didn't arrive you knew one had gone missing; this is just another example of how meticulous he was in everything he did.

Sue

The Peter Oborne programme about Basil was traumatic to watch at first because Dad never discussed the controversy and we didn't know what he thought. My view is that he was always a very honest man who wouldn't be persuaded to stand down. If he wanted Basil in the side, he would stick to it. When the programme found that Dad wanted Bas in the side I was pleased, he wouldn't be influenced if he thought he was right.

He rarely got annoyed as a captain or at home, he was a very placid man. He only smacked me once and then he had to apologise because he was wrong. I was the only one likely to annoy him though; we were very close but could be volatile.

Equally the players knew where they stood. Len Coldwell, Jack Flavell and Jim Standen all knew where they were with Dad as captain. He had the ability to know how people needed to be treated as individuals and would not manage everyone the same. He was aware that some needed shouting at but he was wise and would do it in private.

Lesley

I'm very similar in temperament to Dad. He didn't talk much unless he had something to say, I'm just like that too. I'm calm and if something goes wrong you can rely on me to sort it out. Dad told me he was like that at times; cool on the outside but not on the inside. When I lived in London, he'd come and stay if there was a match or a selection meeting and he confided in me on this occasion and told me about how he felt in these situations.

Martin

He was very analytical and was a meticulously good planner, especially if something had gone wrong he wanted to put it right as soon as possible. He always gave a very balanced, thought-through approach. In short, he was a very good man manager who knew peoples' strengths and weaknesses and realised when they just needed a quiet word.

Sue

It wasn't until I had Dan in 1987 that I really got back into cricket, that's when I met Eric Clapton. Dad was president in Botham's first year. One weekend I took Dan to the ground and heard that Eric, who was a friend of Botham's, was playing in The Crown at Martley. Martin was out and once he found out, he was upset that he couldn't meet one of his heroes. So I went along, smuggled Dan in under my coat and in a back room, there was Clapton, Stan Webb of Chicken Shack fame and the Worcestershire and Essex players. I sat next to Steve Rhodes' mom who rocked Dan away all night.

On another occasion I remember a helicopter landed at the ground and out of it got George Harrison, Elton John, Eric and Jeff Lynne. Dad was the biggest Beatles fan ever and loved having the chance to meet George. For days after it was: '… and I said to George' '… and George said to me', he was thrilled to bits!

They were all in the committee room with Dad sitting among them as president. He was ok with Botham and realised that you had to do anything to keep the club going.

I had had a wonderful evening in the company of the people who knew Don so well. As the evening drew to a close, we diverted our attention to sadder times. On 11 November 1996, Don was due to give a talk and show his home-shot cine film of the world tour of 1965 to the Worcestershire Cricket Society. A packed house had gathered in the Kenyon Room at New Road and was looking forward to the evening as they would any other.

As he stood up to speak, Don collapsed and was rushed to hospital by ambulance where his long-time friend, Martin Horton, was by his side. Don had not been well and was waiting to attend a hospital appointment but alas it came too late and he passed away.

Sue remembers the evening vividly:

I was out with Mom and we were running a bit late, so Dad went to the ground and we arranged to meet him there. Dan was due to go with him, but for some unknown reason, and maybe this is fate, Dad asked for Dan not to accompany him on this particular evening which was totally out of character; it's as if he knew something was going to happen.

The day he died, he said he was not looking forward to doing his talk on the world tour and said, 'People don't realise the stress.' He was shy and found public speaking difficult but this comment proved more telling because it was on the day he died. With all the people looking at him, even though it was a subject he knew so well, he found it difficult. He was confident on the field but off it, he found it much more difficult.

An extract form the obituary in *Wisden* from 1997 quotes teammate and former president, George Chesterton:

Worcester was the only place in the world where 'Don' did not immediately conjure up Bradman. He embarked on a career of run accumulation that hardly ever wavered and opposing bowlers could only stand despairingly as this broad shouldered figure boomed the ball past mid-on or extra cover. Never a talkative or perhaps imaginative man, but his natural seriousness, authority and example made his captaincy successful.

Colin Bateman in the *Daily Express* referred to Don as 'a polished batsman, who relished taking on fast bowlers, he became the heaviest scorer in Worcestershire's history with more than 37,000 runs to his credit.'

Former *Worcester Evening News* Sports Editor, Jack Godfrey, paid his own tribute,

Under his captaincy Worcestershire had not known such glory days nor such support and enthusiasm. Kenyon led his players with tactical wisdom, dignity and respect of all on the county scene.

He shrewdly exploited what was probably the best bowling attack in the County Championship and made brilliant use of his side's batting resources.

Tim Curtis, former opening bat and then County captain, said of Don: 'He was a players' man who loved to see the game played hard and well.'

Former Warwickshire player Jack Bannister recalled how Don once solved a difficult situation in a TCCB disciplinary meeting:

Surrey fast bowler Geoff Arnold was 'on a charge' for using foul and abusive language towards umpire Peter Wight during a Sunday League game at Edgbaston. Peter would not reveal the actual words used and was asked to write them down.

Don, becoming more impatient asked, 'Mr Chairman, did the player use any four letter words and if so did they begin with two letters of the first six in the alphabet?' As soon as Wight nodded, Don replied, 'What are we wasting our time for? He, (pointing at Jack) called me that every time he missed the middle of my bat.'

In the service held in Worcester Cathedral, Club President and long-time friend Tom Graveney paid his own tribute,

Rising from the ranks so to speak, to captain your county was never an easy thing to do, as I found out. But Don took it all in his stride and thrived on it. We had a side of varied temperaments but he handled them all brilliantly and I have no doubt that winning those early Championships in the 60s was down to Don. There was never any fuss or panic and he was always in control – certainly the best captain I played under. He was a wonderful player and a fine man.

Don's name is forever synonymous with success, so in 2001 at the request of the Kenyon family, the Don Kenyon Award was inaugurated. The magnificent silver trophy is presented to the Worcestershire player at the end of each season who has produced the best match winning performance in a first-class game. It was first presented to Andy Bichel for scoring 76 and 37 runs plus bowling of 1 – 72 and 6 – 44 in the 252 run victory over Gloucestershire at Bristol.

The Worcestershire Club's 2001 Yearbook states that the instigation of this award would have been 'music to Don's ears' and no doubt it would have been because success and a desire to be the best in his profession is what drove Don to be, his own man.

Jean presenting the Kenyon Award to Worcestershire legend Graeme Hick in 2004. From the Kenyon family collection

Acknowledgements

I would like to thank the following people who have contributed material for inclusion in this book: John Aldridge, Mike Beddow, Richie Benaud, Roy Booth, Geoffrey Boycott, Terry Church, Ted Dexter, John Elliott, Duncan Fearnley, Grace Fuller, Norman Gifford, Tom Graveney Ron Headley, Graeme Hick, Margaret Horton, Raymond Illingworth, Doug Insole, Derek Isles, Daniel Jackson, Martin Jackson, Sue Jackson, Jeff Jones, Jean Kenyon, Lesley Kenyon, Len Manning, Alan Ormrod, Derek Pearson, Phil Neale, Don Shepherd, M. J. K. Smith, Alf Tasker, Glenn Turner, Mike Vockins, Norman Whiting.

The author and publisher would like to thank the following people/organisations for permission to use copyright material in this book:

Berrows Newspapers (Worcester News)
Mirrorpix
The Black Country Bugle
Derek Pearson
EMPICS PA
Getty Images
The Kenyon family
Coloursport

Every attempt has been made to seek permission for copyright material used in this book. However, if we have inadvertently used copyright material without permission/acknowledgement we apologise and we will make the necessary correction at the first opportunity.

I'm equally grateful to family, friends and colleagues who have guided and supported me through the writing and preparation of this book especially: Richard Bentley, Richard Brown, Sean Cullen, Ross Fletcher, Mike Grundy, Peter Rixon, Patrick Quirke, Jeremy Turner, Ken Workman.

Tim Jones, Wolverhampton 2015

Bibliography

Books

Brown, Freddie, *Cricket Musketeer*, Kaye N., (1954)

Chignell, Wilfred, *History of Worcestershire CCC 1844–1950*, Littlebury & Company, (1954)

Chignell, Wilfred, *History of Worcestershire CCC 1950–1968*, Littlebury & Company, (1968)

Church, Terry, *Lost Cricket and Football Grounds in the South of the Black Country*, TC/BCS Publicatiuons, (2013)

Davis, Alex, *First in the Field – History of Birmingham & District Cricket League*, K A F Brewin Books, (1988)

D'Oliveira, Basil, *D'Oliveira: An Autobiography*, Sportsmans Book Club, (1968)

D'Oliveira, Basil, *The D'Oliveira Affair*, Collins, (1969)

Hatton, Les, *Famous Cricketers Series*, ACS Publications, (2000)

Hatton, Les, *100 Greats – Worcestershire County Cricket Club*, Tempus Publishing Ltd, (2001)

Hignall, Andrew, *Summer of '64*, Tempus, (2005)

Hill, Stan, *Black Country Personalities*, Black Country Society, (2002)

Hutton, Len, *Just My Story*, Hutchinson, London, (1956)

Lemmon, David, *The Official History of Worcestershire County Cricket Club*, Christopher Helm, (1989)

Marshall, Michael, *Gentlemen and Players Conversations with Cricketers*, Grafton Books, (1987)

Oborne, Peter, *Cricket and Conspiracy: The Untold Story*, Little, Brown, (2004)

Ross, Gordon, *The Gillette Cup 1963 to 1908*, Queen Anne Press, (1981)

Thomson, Arthur Alexander, *Cricket the Great Captains*, Stanley Paul (1965)

Vockins, Mike, *Worcestershire County cricket Club: A Pictorial History*, Severn House Publishers, (1980)

Walker, Peter, *It's Not Just Cricket*, Fairfield Books, (2006)

Walsh, Richard, *All Over In a Day*, Richard Walsh Books, (1993)

Wisden Cricketers' *Almanack*, Sporting Handbooks, (1963)

Wisden Cricketers' *Almanack*, John Wisden and Company Ltd, (1997)

Worcestershire County Cricket Club – Club Yearbooks 1947–1997

Newspapers Accessed

Birmingham Gazette
Birmingham Mail
Birmingham Mail Sports Final
Birmingham Post
Boy's Own Paper
Bulawayo Chronicle
County Express
Daily Express
Daily Mail
Daily Mirror
Daily Sketch
Daily Telegraph
East African Standard
Evening Despatch
Evening Mail
Evening News and Times
Honolulu Advertiser, Hawaii
Kidderminster Times
Kidderminster Shuttle
News Chronicle
Saturday Sports Argus
Saturday Sports News
Sporting Buff
Sports Argus
Sunday Chronicle
Sunday Mercury
Sunday Pictorial
Sunday Telegraph
The Star
The Times
The Western Mail
Toowoomba Chronicle, Australia
Wolverhampton, Express and Star
Worcester Evening News
Yorkshire Post and Leeds Mercury

Career statistics (supplied by Les Hatton)

Season by season in all first-class matches (batting and fielding)

Season	Matches	Innings	Not Out	Runs	Highest Score	Average	100	50	Caught
1946	12	19	2	343	107	20.17	1	1	9
1947	29	54	3	1299	152*	25.47	2	2	10
1948	15	28	3	420	46	16.80	-	-	9
1949	30	54	1	1691	182	31.90	1	11	23
1950	32	58	3	2351	163	42.74	6	14	28
1951	32	59	6	2145	145	40.47	6	9	19
1951–52 India, Pakistan & Ceylon	17	29	4	733	112	29.32	1	4	2
1952	34	60	2	2489	171	42.91	7	12	20
1953	32	58	3	2439	258*	44.34	6	17	22
1954	33	58	7	2636	253*	51.68	6	13	17
1955	34	64	3	2296	131	37.63	5	13	18
1956	31	52	3	1994	259	40.69	4	10	13
1957	34	62	3	2231	200*	37.81	6	7	16
1958	24	46	1	1438	107	31.95	2	9	9
1959	30	57	1	1613	229	28.80	5	6	11
1960	31	56	0	1750	201	31.25	5	6	15
1961	30	56	1	1399	152	25.43	2	3	17
1962	33	59	4	1941	106*	35.29	2	14	19
1963	28	49	0	1393	166	28.42	1	11	8
1964	29	52	2	1480	158*	29.60	3	7	17
1964-65 Rhodesia	2	4	0	143	63	35.75	-	1	-
1965	20	33	1	458	77	14.31	-	2	0
1965–66 Jamaica	1	2	0	70	45	35.00	-	-	-
1966	24	41	1	1091	114	27.27	2	3	7
1967	26	49	5	1159	121 *	26.34	1	5	8
TOTAL	643	1159	59	37002	259	33.63	74	180	327